THE VINE STREET IRREGULARS

Frontispiece: The author hamming it up in the former Geography Department Library, Avery Hall, University of Nebraska-Lincoln, 1975/1976.

THE VINE STREET IRREGULARS
A Chronicle of Graduate Student Life and Politics at the University of Nebraska-Lincoln
1975–1976

MICHAEL R. HILL
(*aka* Michael Hilligoss
— *a nom de plume*)

Zea Books
Lincoln, Nebraska
2022

Copyright © 2022 by Michael R. Hill

This book is set in Times New Roman

Front cover: (a) Caricature of the author by a *Daily Nebraskan* staff artist weekly to accompany the weekly dispatches from the Vine Street Irregulars (b) Former entrance hallway to the Department of Geography in Avery Hall where the "Vine Street Irregulars" essays were written

Jane Addams Research Center Publication Series, No. 2

Produced in association with the
Jane Addams Research Center
Mary Jo Deegan, Executive Director
904 Main Street
St. Joseph, Michigan 49085

ISBN 978-1-60962-268-8 paperback
ISBN 978-1-60962-269-5 ebook
DOI:10.32873/unl.dc.zea.1335

Zea Books are published by the
University of Nebraska–Lincoln Libraries.

Electronic (pdf) edition available online at
https://digitalcommons.unl.edu/zeabook/

UNL does not discriminate based upon any protected status.
Please go to http://www.unl.edu/equity/notice-nondiscrimination

This volume is dedicated with every best wish to

ROLLIN R. DAVIS, PH.D.

— Fellow alumnus, congenial colleague, dedicated scholar —

Acknowledgments

This volume owes large debts to Rebecca Brite and Vince Boucher, former editors of the *Daily Nebraskan*, who made space available for the *Vine Street Irregulars* on a weekly basis during the academic year 1975/76. *The Daily Nebraskan* is gratefully acknowledged for permission to republish the material contained herein. Thanks to Kim Jorgensen, Library Service Associate, Lincoln City Libraries, for crucial reference assistance. Additional thanks are due Paul Royster, Rollin Davis, and Mary Jo Deegan.

Given the critical nature of the essays in this volume, I must in counterpoint recognize several professors in whose counsel, courses, seminars, study groups, and independent study projects I met with intellectual maturity, unfettered inquiry, and rigorous reflection. The supportive, cooperative, and creative attitudes of the following instructors turned my graduate (and my recent, on-going post-graduate) studies into wonderful adventures:

Alan P. Bates (Sociology, University of Nebraska-Lincoln)
Brian Blouet (Geography, University of Nebraska-Lincoln)
Miguel Carranza (Sociology, University of Nebraska-Lincoln)
Mary Jo Deegan (Sociology, University of Nebraska-Lincoln)
Betty Dobratz (Sociology, University of Nebraska-Lincoln)
Charles Thomas Elder (Graham School, University of Chicago)
Colbert Held (Geography, University of Nebraska-Lincoln)
Emilie Jane Yardley-Hodges (Writing, School of the Art Institute of Chicago)
James F. Klumpp (Speech Communication, University of Nebraska-Lincoln)
Werner Leinfellner (Philosophy, University of Nebraska-Lincoln)
C. Barron "Mac" McIntosh (Geography, University of Nebraska-Lincoln)
J. Miller McPherson (Sociology, University of Nebraska-Lincoln)
Dale Mesner (Mathematics, University of Nebraska-Lincoln)
Walter E. Mientka (Mathematics, University of Nebraska-Lincoln)
Annie Morse (Art History, School of the Art Institute of Chicago)
Monte Page (Psychology, University of Nebraska-Lincoln)
Amos Rapporort (Anthropology, University of Wisconsin-Milwaukee)
Gwyn Rowley (Geography, University of Nebraska-Lincoln)
Charles Sayward (Philosophy, University of Nebraska-Lincoln)
Robert H. Stoddard (Geography, University of Nebraska-Lincoln)
Philip E. Vogel (Geography, University of Nebraska at Omaha)
Andrew Weigert (Sociology, University of Notre Dame)

Contents

Acknowledgments vi

A Brief Introduction to the Vine Street Irregulars ix

1. The Vine Street Irregulars 1

2. Consumer Advocacy 3

3. The Assist in Assistantships 5

4. Becoming Visible 7

5. Student Club or Representative Assembly? 9

6. Yossarian Writes a Letter 11

7. Bureaucracy Recognition Day: A Documentary 13

8. Sue the Bastards? 15

9. Choosing a Graduate Program 17

10. Apathy, Fear, and Administrative Complacency 19

11. The Plastic Suit Gang 21

12. Inferior Photocopies 23

13. Campus as Symbol 27

14. Censure the President of the Faculty Senate 29

15. Putting Grad Skills to Work 31

16. Welcome Back 33

17. Meeting Leonik 35

18. Coffee Economics 37

19. Clear the Decks! 39

20. Lessons from the Faculty Union Vote 41

21. Bereuter's Scapegoats 43

22. The Job Market 45

23. Real Politics 47

24. Organization and Its Pitfalls 49

25. *e pluribus interim* 51

26. Search Committees 53

27. A Farewell Letter 55

———————

Appendix I: Selected Letters, Responses, and a Caricature 57

Appendix II: *DN* Writer Now Sociology Prof — Rebellious 1970's Columnist Has Become Respected Scholar
Elizabeth Polles 61

———————

About the Author 63

A Brief Introduction to the Vine Street Irregulars

I proposed writing these imaginary dispatches from the Vine Street Irregulars during the 1975–1976 academic year, for publication in the *Daily Nebraskan*, a student newspaper at the University of Nebraska-Lincoln. Rebecca Brite, the Editor of the *Daily Nebraskan*, not only accepted my proposal, but also allowed me the unusual courtesy of using a *nom de plume*: "Michael Hilligoss." A note appended by Brite to the inaugural dispatch stated publicly:

> *Hilligoss is "an old family name" claimed by Michael Hill,*
> *a Ph.D. student in geography. His reports from the*
> *VSI underground will appear every Wednesday.*

But this note, apparently, went largely unnoticed and "Michael Hilligoss" took on more reality than I expected (see Appendix I).

Were Hilligoss, Yossarian, Leonik, the Vine Street Irregulars and their activities *real*? To the extent that several people wrote serious letters to them in care of the *Daily Nebraskan*, they were real. To the extent that every café, restaurant, dining room, and bar mentioned in the reports were actual establishments frequented by Nebraska graduate students, they were real. To the extent that their reports and criticisms gave more than one administrator heartburn, they were real. And, to the extent that each report reflected true events and situations, albeit sometimes disguised to protect the vulnerable, they were again very real. And yes, "Hilligoss" was my father's surname until he shortened it legally — so that too was real.

Many changes have visited the Lincoln campus since 1976, some positive, some regrettably regressive, and I since moved on to other pursuits (see Appendix II). In retrospect, I am struck that so many of the cafés and watering holes we frequented as graduate students are no longer extant — or are now so remodeled as to be unrecognizable. Long hours of scholarly debate, gossip, and rowdy horseplay over beers with my fellow students in the Department of Geography are anchored in my memory to several of Lincoln's seedier taverns, now gone. Indeed, the Department's 1970s home, in Avery Hall, has been replaced by Mathematics and Computer Science. It is unsettling that the physical complexion of a university can change so quickly, discarding the pregnant, particular milieus that make a campus a vivid and dynamic experience for each new cohort of graduate students.

If I reach further back — to 1967 — to my first formal semester as a graduate student on the Lincoln campus, great chunks of sheer placedness now remain only in my memory. The bowed slate stairs and time-etched walls of the old Geography Building (once the State Museum), are physically gone. The *real* Cornhusker Hotel (where Mari Sandoz, long before I came to Lincoln, sat for hours nursing cups of coffee and writing her distinctive prose) — *gone*. And if I stretch even further back, to 1960, I recall standing with other highschool students on the grassy "Knothole" section of Memorial Stadium to watch a Nebraska football game for 50¢, that era too is long since past.

The old Nebraska Bookstore, Akademia, the Campus Bookstore (then all on "R" Street) where we browsed the shelves for new and out-of-print titles, *all gone*. A comprehensive list of decay, disappearances, and distortions is too long to report here, but one conclusion is clear. We homesteaded our own patch of campus space-time, knowing that change would come, of course, but not understanding then that the apparently solid, immediate world we once inhabited together as graduate students remains today largely in our memories, not extant on the ground.

The memories recalled in the twenty-seven essays in the volume are anchored in sometimes intense and sometimes admittedly naive graduate student experiences at the University of Nebraska-Lincoln during the 1970's. Master's degree in hand, I returned to graduate study at Nebraska in 1972 after four years in the military, benefitting not only from the G.I. Bill, but also from a National Defense Education Act Fellowship. I was increasingly wise to the ways of administrative bureaucrats who were sometimes enlightened, sometimes punitive, draconian, and exploitive, or — far more often — simply moribund. As adult students, we wanted fair play and respect. I pursued those goals at Nebraska as: (a) the Geography Department representative to the University Graduate Student Association, (b) as an early vice-president of the Graduate Student Association, (c) as UNL's graduate student voting member on the three-campus System Graduate Council, (d) as a voting member on two Vice-Chancellor Search Committees, and finally (e) as the UNL Graduate Student Representative investigating and voting on a fellow graduate student's formal (and contentious) grade appeal. In these various roles, many students told me stories that made my toes curl. The cumulative result was a hands-on tutorial in bureaucratic/administrative machinations as they ground onward day after day on the Nebraska campuses. Subsequently, writing the essays that became *The Vine Street Irregulars* gave me a way to explore, in public, the issues, problems, and experiences that bedeviled the lives of far too many graduate students on the University of Nebraska campus during the mid 1970s. Now, nearly fifty years later, this volume preserves some of those struggles and hopefully captures parts of the socio-spatial milieu in which they unfolded. Minor errors and a few awkward phrases have been silently repaired. Where potentially useful, explanatory footnotes are appended.

— MRH

The Vine Street Irregulars [1]

MICHAEL HILLIGOSS

THE VINE STREET IRREGULARS[2] have recently come to my attention through a personal acquaintance known within that underground graduate student organization by the code name "Yossarian."[3] Having given him my assurance that his anonymity will be preserved, it is now possible for me to report to you on the secret operations of this little-known, loose-knit group of rebels within the University of Nebraska.

In this first report I can give only a limited sketch of the objectives and organizational structure of the Vine Street Irregulars, but in future columns I will present further details of the charges made by the Vine Street Irregulars against the University and its lackeys.

The Vine Street Irregulars, as I have come to understand from Yossarian, are composed of a handful of disillusioned but capable graduate students who are dedicated to freedom of speech and action within graduate life and education at the University. They are opposed to all forms of academic repression and administrative rip-off. In future reports I will review several case studies of problems that have been identified and researched by the secret, investigative arm of the Vine Street Irregulars.

The group functions through an informal network of interdepartmental contacts. Yossarian tells me that one or two members of the Vine Street Irregulars can usually be found in every academic department with a graduate program at the University. Formal organization is apparently made impossible by the fear (real or imagined) of departmental and University retaliation. With this fear of reprisal heavy on his mind, Yossarian asked that I help give widespread publication and

---

[1] *Daily Nebraskan*, 20 August 1975, p. 4.

[2] The name played on "the Baker Street Irregulars," the fictitious group of street urchins recruited by Sherlock Holmes, and introduced in Arthur Conan Doyle's *A Study in Scarlet*, to perform various missions, collect clues, and go places where the famous detective himself could not. Vine Street *per se* is a major east-west thoroughfare in north Lincoln that leads directly to the heart of the University of Nebraska city campus and terminated in what was then a large parking area near Memorial Stadium, the home of "Big Red" football.

[3] The name "Yossarian" echoed a character in Joseph Heller's absurdist novel, *Catch-22*.

discussion to the allegations made by the Vine Street Irregulars against the University.

Yossarian is convinced that the majority of graduate students will feel considerable sympathy with the aims of the Vine Street Irregulars—once the issues have been clearly presented. Although I could not assure him that Nebraska students will be responsive, I have agreed to conclude each forthcoming report with Yossarian's concrete proposals for individual student action in concert with the general aims of the Vine Street Irregulars.

Editor's [4] Note: Hilligoss is "an old family name" claimed by Michael Hill, a Ph.D. student in geography. His reports from the VSI underground will appear every Wednesday.

---

[4] Rebecca Brite edited the *Daily Nebraskan*.

■ 2 ■

Consumer Advocacy (Observer gives student tips for cracking bureaucracy)[5]

"YOSSARIAN" met with me at the Brass Rail[6] last Saturday and we discussed further the program and tactics of the Vine Street Irregulars, a small, loose-knit band of disenchanted graduate students at the University of Nebraska.

I had hoped to impress Yossarian with my deep interest in the aims of the Vine Street Irregulars by telling him about a recent "unpleasantness" I experienced at the hands of a University bureaucrat and the (I thought) militant manner in which I had confronted the situation. To my surprise, Yossarian became agitated as I related the incident, observed that I was still very much an amateur, and concluded that my handling of the situation probably did more to bolster my ego than to effect any permanent resolution helpful to others facing similar situations. Yossarian surmised that you usually can't accomplish much in verbal exchanges with underlings and low-level clerks.

"It does no good to call the attention of the underpaid student worker at the Library circulation desk to the gross inappropriateness of the exorbitant over-due book fine with which you are faced," he said penuriously.

"And, you can raise the rafters about poorly taught courses, but it probably won't do much good if the rafters aren't ringing around a dean's head somewhere," he continued.

Yossarian explained that every "difficult situation" is unique and that even experienced Vine Street Irregulars learn to respond expertly only with practice.

He added, however, that there are five fundamental tactics for confronting bureaucrats that anyone, even undergraduates, can learn and use:

First, don't waste your time. Always ascertain at the outset whether or not the persons to whom you are talking have the authority to correct the undesirable situations to which you have called their attention. If they don't, find out who their supervisors are and go see them.

Second, stand your ground once you locate the appropriate decision-making level and be prepared for such ploys as, "Yes, that's a good point but you must

---

[5] *Daily Nebraskan*, 27 August 1975, p. 4. The parenthetical sub-titles were added each week by the editorial staff of the *Daily Nebraskan*.

[6] The Brass Rail Tavern, 1436 "O" Street

understand how difficult it is to change something like this in a system as complex as a large university."

Third, if higher-up administrators persist in avoiding the immediacy or the importance of the issue, ask to see *their* supervisors. Be prepared to go to the top, step by step.

Fourth, when confronted with the ploy, "Well, what's your alternative?" remember that you are not obliged to do the administrators' work for them. Devising solutions to problems are what administrators get paid for—handsomely.

Fifth, after finally talking to a responsible administrator, follow up everything in a written letter. State, in your letter, that you are serious and are prepared to take the issue higher if the problem is not satisfactorily resolved.

Explain also that: (1) you have kept a copy of your letter, for future reference, (2) you expect a prompt response within a stated and reasonable time period, and (3) you are sending information copies to the Ombudsman, a family lawyer, or some trustworthy public official, such as your state Legislator, for their files.

I told Yossarian he sounded more like a consumer advocate than a grad student rebel.

"Of course," he replied. "Remember that check you wrote last week for tuition and fees? That's *our* money that buys the University's red tape, inefficiency, and incompetence. We're paying for the instruments of our own frustration. Sometimes we should think a lot more like consumers. Demand your money's worth!"

■ 3 ■

The Assist in Assistantships (Yossarian wants assist put back in assistantships) [7]

"YOU look a bit glum," I said to Yossarian as we found a table in the warm, red glow at Cliff's.[8] Without actually giving an affirmative reply, my informant related that a few Vine Street Irregulars were unable to return to graduate school this fall.

"Their assistantships were terminated," he said with a sigh, "not because they were poor students but because they were poor teachers."

I told Yossarian I didn't understand what being a good teacher had to do with getting financial aid for graduate school if an individual was a good student and had excellent grades.

"Teaching has nothing to do with getting aid initially," he said, "but it often has everything to do with keeping it." He explained that a student is "awarded" a teaching assistantship (or "TA") primarily on his academic potential as a *scholar*, but that the yearly renewal of the "award" frequently depends more on his performance as a *teacher*, especially in departments that are sensitive to enrollments.

Unfortunately, Yossarian noted, grad students can't always do justice to their coursework and their teaching duties at the same time. It's difficult to do an outstanding job as both scholar and teacher if you are required to take at least nine hours of graduate work while also assuming full-course teaching responsibility for as many as six credit hours in freshman and sophomore-level classes.

"While most grad students feel an enormous responsibility for the classes they teach, some put more emphasis on their own coursework," Yossarian concluded. "After all, big surprise, most grad students come here *to study*, not to become teachers—and many will never teach again after they get their graduate degrees.

"This problem becomes especially serious when the graduate student who is a capable scholar has neither aptitude nor appetite for teaching," he said.

"Although Nebraska freshmen sometimes find themselves taught by inexperienced TAs,"[9] Yossarian observed, "the economics of the TA funding system

---

[7] *Daily Nebraskan*, 3 September 1975, p. 4.

[8] Cliff's Cocktail Lounge, lower level, underneath Cliff's Smoke Shop, 1204 "O" Street.

[9] It can get worse. To cut instructional costs, a few Nebraska departments have in recent years assigned *undergraduate* seniors to some classrooms as instructors.

allows the 'regular' faculty members to afford something they really want—the prestige and lighter teaching loads of a graduate program.

"Each department needs to have as many lower-level courses and labs taught as cheaply as possible so that the senior faculty can devote themselves to teaching graduate courses.

"TAs provide the financial slack in what would otherwise be prohibitively expensive programs and, at the same time, provide the resident warm bodies who enroll in each department's ego-conscious graduate programs. Quite a trick, huh?"

"Is there a solution for the TA's dual and often conflicting commitments to both teaching and scholarship?" I asked.

Yossarian noted that a possible answer lies in setting up a couple of University-wide teaching/funding programs. First, the University could allocate a few part-time teaching positions to each department via a hiring plan *monitored by the University's personnel department*. Yossarian convinced me that individuals who are hired as part-time teachers should be qualified to teach and should receive the full benefits of University employment. Each job should be advertised and filled in accordance with equal opportunity rules. "Given the relatively low level of pay and the part-time nature of these jobs, it should be obvious that many applicants will also be potential part-time graduate students," Yossarian observed, "but the idea is to insure that classroom instructors are actually qualified teachers."

Second, Yossarian urged, the University should also allocate a few part-time "assistance" grants to each department in a program *monitored by the Graduate College*. "A student who is awarded an 'assistance' grant should be required to do only that—*assist*—not assume full-course responsibilities," said Yossarian. "The primary criterion for renewing these grants should be outstanding performance as a scholar."

Yossarian suggested that the best way to get action on creative solutions to "the TA problem" is to start talking to the people who can make the changes. Rigorous change would be good for both graduates and undergraduates at the University.

"Invite your dean for a cup of coffee," he counseled. "Many deans actually enjoy talking to students once in a while."

"I will," I said, and thanked him for reminding me that a dean is someone students should feel free to talk to.

■ 4 ■

Becoming Visible (Forgotten grad students seek increased visibility)[10]

"YOSSARIAN," I said, "did you know people have actually been asking me if you exist, if you're *real*?"

"Not surprising," he said, raising his glass in salutation to Casey's[11] Tuesday Night crowd.

"You know," he continued, "what's much more interesting is that the existence of the Vine Street Irregulars itself is often questioned. It seems that the faculty—and the administration generally—regard it as incredible that a small group of graduate students from different departments could find anything in common.

"And the Vine Street Irregulars are few in number," he added. "Do you realize that if the Vine Street Irregulars had 100 members (which we don't) that would only be about three percent of the graduate student body."

"But the part about having members from almost every department," I pursued., "isn't that a bit much to ask people to believe?"

"Is that so unusual?" he asked. "Every discipline is represented in the Faculty Senate. Is it so hard to understand that graduate students have at least as many common concerns as the faculty?"

"Nevertheless, Yossarian, you must admit that graduate students don't have much visibility as a group," I countered.

"Our numbers do seem to be repressed somewhere deep in the administration's subconscious," he surmised. "In fact," he said, "more than 3,000 grad students were registered at Nebraska last semester. *That's one grad student for every five undergraduates."*

"But if there really are that many graduate students on campus," I said, "surely the special needs of a group that size would come to the attention of the administration?"

"Quite the contrary, Hilligoss," he chastised, "things run much more smoothly if administrators pretend that graduate students—*as a group*—don't exist. Consider the changes that might be called for if anyone took effective notice of our collective existence. Think of it," he encouraged. "There would be proposals for an off-campus graduate student lounge, apartment-style housing, the unionization of

---

[10] *Daily Nebraskan*, 10 September 1975, p. 4.

[11] Casey's Beverage, 1020 "P" Street.

teaching assistants, extended library hours, published evaluations of the graduate faculty, and so on.[12] What administrator wants to deal with proposals like that? Too many meetings, too much paperwork, too many headaches! It's much easier for administrators to forget about Nebraska graduate students as a category.

"For example," he said, "even though grad students do most of the research on this campus (theses, dissertations, seminar papers, etc.), the campus library doesn't know what proportion of its total book circulation is due to grad student use. We check out thousands of volumes, but we're invisible as a user class.

"Or, take the Comptroller's office. They have no idea how much money grad students kick into the student activities fund when we pay our fees each term.

"Yes," he lamented, "we are doing much of the active research, a lot of the teaching and most of the serious studying, but we're much less visible than the incoming freshmen.[13] Statistically, we're just lumped in with all the undergraduates even though our demographic profile differs sharply. We're older and more mature, we have BA and MA degrees, many of us are married and have children, a lot of us are veterans, and as TAs a lot of us are University employees."

"Is there an answer to the administration's myopia?" I asked.

"For a start, stand up and be counted," Yossarian suggested. "Don't be apologetic about being a graduate student, we're not an anomaly! Remind each administrator (when you have occasion to talk to one) that there are real and meaningful differences between the needs of undergraduate and graduate students. Do this frequently and—who knows?—someone in the administration might just take notice."

---

[12] Such facilities and activities were commonplace on many other campuses at the time. And when I saw some wonderfully-appointed Graduate Student Club buildings on rival campuses, I was truly envious. In the interim, apartment-style housing has been provided at Nebraska, but little else.

[13] It's worse now. Nebraska now hosts a day-long "welcome bash" each August geared specifically to incoming freshmen, with rock bands, and free prizes and gifts from participating merchants. There is little if any school-wide institutional recognition of new graduate students per se.

■ 5 ■

Student Club or Representative Assembly? (UNL grad students left out; UNO group collects money) [14]

WITH a roast beef sandwich in one hand and an Oly in the other, Yossarian ushered me to a corner table at Lebsack's.[15]

"You know, Hilligoss," he said as we sat down, "I was serious when I said last week that graduate students should stand up and be counted. There's too much money at stake just to sit idly by." Yossarian explained that "standing up to be counted" is, unfortunately, the only way graduate students can get a direct return on the student activity fees they are required to pay every semester.

"Do you realize," he asked, "that the organization representing the 2,100 grad students at the University of Nebraska at Omaha got $1,350 in funding last year while the 3,100 grad students in Lincoln received only $400? And this year," he continued, "the Omaha grads received $1,100 whereas the grads in Lincoln got nothing at all!"

"That's quite a discrepancy," I said. "What's the problem?"

"Apparently the Nebraska Graduate Student Association in Lincoln didn't ask the campus Fees Allocation Board for funds this year," replied Yossarian. "They never stood up to be counted."

"Should they really have to ask?" I questioned. "Isn't it coming to them without their having to make a formal request every year?"

"You would think so," said Yossarian, "but in Lincoln the Graduate Student Association is treated as though it's just another undergraduate activity club when it comes to funding. Rather than recognizing the Graduate Student Association for what it is—the officially chartered representative assembly of 3,500 graduate students—it is treated no differently than a small club with a handful of members. The funding apparatus simply does not appreciate that each so-called 'member' is actually a duly elected representative of a campus graduate program," he observed.[16] "They just can't figure it out—or don't want to."

---

[14] *Daily Nebraskan*, 17 September 1975, p. 4.

[15] Lebsack's, 220 North 10th Street, then famous for braunsweiger sandwiches.

[16] The Executive Graduate Council chartered the GSA but provided no operating funds. Thus, the GSA in Lincoln was forced to stand in line, hat in hand, to vie for funds with dozens of undergraduate clubs in a competitive process administered by the campus Fees Allocation Board, an organization constitutionally dominated by undergraduate students.

"It's time to change the situation," said Yossarian. "I'm asking all Vine Street Irregulars to encourage the graduate students in their respective departments to send sharp, tough-minded representatives to the GSA, representatives who are willing to jump through bureaucratic hoops when needed and who will stand up to be reckoned with when our collective interests are at stake."

"That's rather stirring, even inspirational," I said. "Do you think anyone will listen to the urging of the Vine Street Irregulars?"

"Well, the GSA is due to collect at least two to three thousand dollars if it presents its case in the approved bureaucratic manner. That should be enough money to get the attention of at least a few graduate students," Yossarian winked, "we could do a lot with that kind of money," as he finished the last mouthful of his sandwich.

■ 6 ■

Yossarian Writes a Letter (Law and graduate students share library policy plight)[17]

YOSSARIAN suggested that we meet for lunch at The Palms,[18] where he expected, from all reports, that a tasty meal would be expertly served in a genuinely charming atmosphere. Although the service was terrible and the fried rice a disaster, the delightful decor of the place inspired Yossarian to dash off the following note of greeting to his comrades in the College of Law — while we waited an interminable twenty-five minutes for our orders to be taken:

> Dear Law Students,
> Welcome to the library system at the University of Nebraska. As students within the University library family, you are now learning what most graduate students at Nebraska have always known—the library system cares little about your particular needs or study habits.
> It was warming to see at least a token demonstration of your dissatisfaction with the change in library policy which drastically affects your study and research patterns. You made enough noise that even the *Lincoln Journal* took notice and sided with your cause. The *Journal* was, understandably, at a loss to understand how a library system could deny the requests of students who want only the opportunity to study and do research.
> The *Journal* may not understand, but those of us who have lived with the University of Nebraska libraries as graduate students were not surprised.
> It is unfortunate that our library system does not plan for or take notice of variations in user needs. Quite the opposite attitude is recommended in a Purdue University study by Philip Rzasa and John Moriarty which appeared in the November 1970 issue of *College and Research Libraries*.[19]

---

[17] *Daily Nebraskan,* 24 September 1975, p. 4.

[18] The Palms, 235 North 11th Street, garden level.

[19] Philip V. Rzasa and John H. Moriarty, "The Types and Needs of Academic Library Users: A Case Study of 6,568 Responses," pp. 403-409.

In their study, "Types and Needs of Academic Library Users," Rzasa and Moriarty suggest: "It is desirable to identify functionally different user groups, not only to gauge library effectiveness but also to guide its programs."

Although graduate students and undergraduates are now lumped together in the University of Nebraska library lending code, there is evidence that these two groups have quite different library needs, just as law students have different needs. In the study cited above, Rzasa and Moriarty reported: "The graduate student group and the undergraduates were not homogeneous with respect to their reasons for coming to the library, nor in the library materials which they used."

What we need at Nebraska is the identification of special user groups, combined with imaginative and comprehensive planning for their sometimes disparate needs.

The Vine Street Irregulars are sympathetic to your library plight and lend their support. You are to be congratulated for bringing the issue of special library needs to the surface.

Of course, we hope the special requirements of the much larger group of 3,600 graduate students are not forgotten during the search for a solution to the needs of 470 law students.

In any event, keep up the good fight! And again, welcome to the system.

— Yossarian

■ 7 ■

Bureaucracy Recognition Day: A Documentary (Hands of bureaucracy defy grad students) [20]

I HAD agreed to meet Yossarian at Oscar's[21] but my Vine Street Irregulars informant didn't appear on schedule. An hour and a couple of Bloody Marys later, I saw him puffing up the stairs with a large brown parcel under his arm.

"What do you have there?" I asked as he sat down.

"Oh, you'll be interested," he said. "These are the posers for the Vine Street Irregulars's annual University Bureaucracy Recognition Day."

"Fascinating," I said dryly. "Is there some sort of program or demonstration scheduled?"

"Yes, this year we are planning a dramatization," he answered.

I prompted him, "Some sort of cynical put-down, I suppose?"

"Not at all," he said, "quite the contrary. We're doing a factual documentary about a Nebraska grad student's losing battle with bureaucracy and red tape."

"Can you give me a preview?" I asked.

"Sure," he said, handing me a neatly typed synopsis, which read as follows:

Scene One: Bureaucracy's right hand awards a graduate student (hereafter called "GS") a so-called "double" assistantship,[22] which entails teaching 11 credit hours with full course responsibility. (Technical note: A "double" assistantship usually means twice as much work for considerably less than double the pay).

Scene Two: Bureaucracy's left hand discovers GS's "good" fortune and rules that no TA (double or not) is permitted to teach that many hours.

Scene Three: Bureaucracy's right hand solves this problem by changing GS's title (but not his work load or salary) from teaching assistant to *part-time* instructor.

---

[20] *Daily Nebraskan*, 1 October 1975, p. 4.

[21] Oscar's Lounge, 245 North 13th Street.

[22] The so-called "double" assistantship; this widely used term had no official standing and was never used in formal letters of appointment. Technically, a student was awarded only one assistantship, but the dollar stipend and the hours of required work could vary substantially not only between departments but also within departments. More recently, a few "fortunate" students were appointed to a new variety of exploitation, the one-year "beginning instructorship," in which former students virtually become full-fledged, full-time members of the faculty but teach heavier course loads and fewer privileges than do their better-paid elders and their same-age colleagues *with the same qualifications* who have been appointed to tenure-leading positions.

The left hand then rules that it's legal for GS to teach 11 credit hours because his title has been changed.

Scene Four: The left hand of bureaucracy informs GS that while TAs get paid in 10 monthly installments beginning in August, instructors (whether full or part-time) get paid in nine monthly installments beginning in September. Because GS was already paid in August as a TA, it is now necessary to *deduct* that August payment from GS's September check as an instructor.

Scene Five: Although GS now has no money, the right hand of bureaucracy appears at the door exclaiming that the tuition payment is due. (Technical note: since GS is in reality still a graduate student and not really a faculty member, he is trying to register for classes and get through graduate school). The left hand tries to cover up this mess by arranging an interest-free loan for GS with which he can then make his tuition payment.

Scene Six: In desperation, GS takes the loan but discovers that he will have less money than he planned on with which to pay back the loan. Because GS is now formally an instructor and is technically an actual member of the faculty, the right hand rules that several deductions to which TAs are not subject (such as social security taxes), must now be deducted from GS's monthly check. *Voilá*, less money for GS!

Epilogue: GS, now in debt, with less pay, and still over-worked, sits at his desk with his studies and course preparations opened before him. His numbed mind tries in vain to remember the campus Ombudsman's[23] phone number. *Curtain.*

"But, Yossarian," I protested, "You said this would be a factual story, not a parody."

"But this isn't at all exaggerated," he said. "It's happening to a Nebraska grad student this fall, right now, in just this way."[24]

"No one will believe you," I said. "People will think you made it up."

"Hilligoss," chided Yossarian, "you should realize by now, after all I've told you, that life as a Nebraska graduate student is almost always stranger than fiction."

---

[23] The campus Ombudsman; an exceptionally useful office, to which anyone, student, staff, or faculty, could—without fear of retaliation—appeal for help and request an anonymous investigation. Unfortunately, the Ombudsman's office was subsequently disbanded, purportedly for budgetary reasons. It has since been revived in various guises, but with much less independence or effectiveness.

[24] The victim of this bureaucratic nightmare was, at the time, a graduate student in the Department of Modern Languages. It is a true story and not in any way exaggerated.

■ 8 ■

Sue the Bastards? (Lawsuits not only answer) [25]

UNABLE to find an uncrowded tavern on Friday night, we made our way up "O" Street to Harry's Wonder Bar.[26] We kept our conversation low, so as not to disturb the sullen members of the silent majority who patronize Harry's place, and who viewed our arrival with disapproval.

"Yossarian," I said, "I understand that a few students are contemplating lawsuits against their departments for giving them the screw in their graduate programs. That's really showing them, isn't it?"

"Maybe so, maybe not," mused Yossarian. "Pursuing a lawsuit when the problem could be settled by other means is irresponsible and damages the injured party's credibility as a scholar."

"But how can a grad student get an impartial hearing if he doesn't go to court?" I asked.

"Slow down, Hilligoss," Yossarian replied. "If the issue is primarily related to the student's employment as a teaching assistant, the student might eventually be forced to the courts because no well-defined procedure exists within the University for resolving teaching assistant disputes.

"But, on the other hand," he said, "why should students expect a fair hearing in the courts on strictly academic or intellectual issues? Can they assume that judges are qualified to rule on such matters?

"Besides," he continued, "several mechanisms within the University are designed to help solve problems with academic programs. And, these mechanisms frequently encourage grad student input.

"For example, if grad students cannot reach an agreement with their advisors and/or committees, they can take their cases to the full graduate committee of their department."

"But what chance do they have there?" I asked.

"More than you might think. It's not widely known," he replied, "but graduate students can be appointed as full voting members of the graduate committee in their respective departments. If given departments have not as yet made such

---

[25] *Daily Nebraskan*, 8 October 1975, p. 4.

[26] Harry's Wonder Bar, 1621 "O" St. Elsewhere, "O" street would be called "Main Street." It is the major east-west line of division between north and south Lincoln. It is pronounced "Oh" as in the letter "O," although some wags call it "Zero Street," not totally without reason.

appointments, students in that department are encouraged by the Vine Street Irregulars to start asking why not, and to press for change. But the department isn't the only place to go for help.

"Each year, a few students are justified in going beyond their departments," added Yossarian.

"In these cases, students can appeal to the Campus Graduate Council, which includes faculty members from several departments, the Dean of the Graduate College and two graduate student members selected by the University-wide Graduate Student Association.

"And, if students still feel that the issue wasn't satisfactorily resolved, they can then go to the Executive Graduate Council, which includes faculty members and grad students from the University of Nebraska at Omaha, the University of Nebraska Medical Center, and the Lincoln campus.

"It's my observation that the graduate councils, if not always the departments, usually make fair, unbiased decisions," Yossarian noted. "Let's face it, if grad students still feel they are being screwed after all those review procedures, they ought to take a good look in the mirror. Besides, lawsuits cost *lots* of money, money probably better spent in transferring to another school and starting over."

■ 9 ■

Choosing a Graduate Program (Advice for the grad worn)[27]

YOSSARIAN surveyed the sea of undergraduates at Sam's[28] with a reflective, philosophical look.

"You look thoughtful," I said. "What's on your mind?"

"You realize, don't you, that a lot of these students will be going blindly on to graduate school next fall?" he responded.

"I suppose so," I said. "But why do you say 'blindly'?"

"Because they won't have thought much about their plans. They'll probably just go to the first place that accepts them, or to the one that offers the most money to become a teaching assistant," he observed.

"Yossarian, you've been through the wars. What advice would you give them?" I prompted.

"Actually, any students serious about grad school should talk with the faculty and the Vine Street Irregulars in their major department," he replied.

And then he added this general advice:

(1) You should identify your motives for going to graduate school. Be certain you really want to attend. Going to graduate school is like getting married, joining a religious order and becoming an apprentice in a medieval craft guild, all at once. You should understand that grad school does not necessarily insure higher salaries or better jobs. As a general rule, grad school is best suited for those who are prepared to dedicate themselves to a scholarly life — at low pay.

(2) Do your homework early. The reference librarians at the library can help you identify schools offering good programs in your major area of interest. Find out about the character and national reputation of the schools that sound promising (and remember, a high ranking in the "Big 8"[29] can mean next to nothing).

(3) Write to attractive schools and ask for detailed information, including faculty strengths and a list of courses offered in upcoming years. Ask specifically about any "special requirements" they may have (such as math or foreign language

---

[27] *Daily Nebraskan*, 15 October 1975, p.4

[28] Sam's, 440 South 11th Street, subsequently Duggan's, now closed.

[29] An *athletic* conference in which athletic and intellectual prowess were often conflated and confused by sports fans and university officials alike; the "Big 8" universities were: Nebraska, Colorado, Iowa State, Kansas, Kansas State, Missouri, Oklahoma, and Oklahoma State. Nebraska next joined the Big 12, and most recently, the curiously named "Big 10".

requirements) so that you can get them out of the way before you leave your undergraduate program. Otherwise, you might be admitted "with deficiencies" and be always playing catch-up.

(4) Begin to consider advisers. The character, focus and rigor of your thesis or dissertation will depend to a great extent on the personality and expertise of your adviser. Read and study the recent work of the faculty members in the school of your choice. Decide before you go if you are comfortable with the foci, philosophies and methodological approaches offered by one or more members of the faculty. In many ways, finding a good adviser is more important than finding a "good" school.

(5) Visit the campus. You are looking for a place to spend the next few years and several thousands of your dollars. Would you buy a house or marry someone, sight unseen? You ought to be at least as choosy when selecting a graduate school.

(6) Apply, if you think it's a place where you'll be comfortable.

(7) Of all the places where you get accepted — and there will be more than one if you have a solid academic record — choose the most rigorous and demanding program that you think you can live with, even if you have to take out a loan or work part-time off campus to cover the expense.

* * * * *

I believe I have everything down here as Yossarian gave it to me, but the din at Sam's was so loud I could barely concentrate.

"I think you're getting old, Hilligoss," said Yossarian, and he promised a quieter setting for our next meeting.

■ 10 ■

Apathy, Fear, and Administrative Complacency (Apathy hides fear of repression) [30]

AS I EASED into a comfortable, overstuffed chair at The Library[31] I could see that Yossarian was irritated.

"What gives?" I began.

"I'm tired of hearing about the supposed 'apathy' of grad students at the University of Nebraska," he said.

"But I've heard they *are* apathetic," I responded. "Just look at the inactivity of the Graduate Student Association."

"You should believe differently," he answered, making the following points:

"A charge of 'apathy' is an easy 'out' for deans, chairs and other administrators who daily shirk their responsibility for improving graduate student life at the University of Nebraska. If, for example, the GSA is less than dynamic, the administrators can wash their hands of any personal responsibility to support this important—but fragile—institution *by blaming student apathy*. The GSA was established—by the Executive Graduate Council—to help guide graduate student affairs, but the GSA cannot fulfill its chartered role if department chairs pretend not to recognize its significance, do not encourage student participation, do not schedule elections, and do not lend secretarial staff assistance.

"For the most part," observed Yossarian, "the grads at Nebraska are anything but apathetic. You should better call them *uninformed* about their rights and understandably fearful of reprisals. Apathy implies insensitivity to what is going on around you," he continued. "But grads at Nebraska have become so sensitive to awful tales of repression that many dare not act publicly in support of their rights lest they jeopardize their degrees and future careers.

"This reign of intimidation results from an administrators' conspiracy of complacency," he charged. "We get a lot of nice speeches, but no one takes responsibility for house cleaning the graduate programs. For example—

---

[30] *Daily Nebraskan*, 22 October 1975, p. 4.

[31] The Library, in the Clocktower East shopping center, 6891 "A" Street, known for comfortable, living room-style seating.

"The system level tells us that the top-heavy tenure level at Nebraska is satisfactory. This closes the door on the chance to replace ineffective professors, or at least add some much-needed new blood.[32]

"The Executive Graduate Council, while chartering the GSA, is unwilling to police the retention of Graduate Faculty Fellow status by professors who are no longer qualified to direct contemporary research.

"The Graduate College quotes the official rules with élan, but it rarely supervises or reviews the *informal* rules that are adopted within many departments.

"The deans of the individual colleges are too concerned with undergraduate credit-hour production to worry seriously about the quality of graduate programs.

"The overall result," he concluded, "is that the graduate programs in many departments are virtually unsupervised by any higher authority. Chairs and department graduate committees are free to break or bend almost any official rule stipulated in the *Graduate Catalog*. Many departmental 'rules' are 'unofficial' and never come to light unless vulnerable students risk their careers and their funding to bring them to the attention of those who are in position to ride herd on maverick departments.[33]

"The end product of the administrators' complacency conspiracy is frustration and pain for many graduate students. Call the Vine Street Irregulars almost anything you want," he concluded, "but do not call us apathetic!"

---

[32] Tenure remains a fundamentally central safeguard for free speech and academic freedom in this increasingly conservative nation, but as a side-effect it also protects unproductive deadwood. While preserving tenure, the University must find creative ways to motivate those key professors who have neither revised their seminar notes nor published anything of substance during the past twenty years.

[33] At my instigation, and with the support of the Graduate Student Association, the Executive Graduate Council issued a directive requiring all departments to prepare an annual set of *Guidelines for Graduate Study* in which all "informal" standards and practices regarding graduate student conduct and performance must be clearly stated. The departmental *Guidelines*, however, are not reviewed by the Graduate College. Thus, the sometimes extreme variance between the *Guidelines* and the regulations stated in the official Graduate Catalog remains a potentially live issue.

■ 11 ■

The Plastic Suit Gang (Red suits conceal profits) [34]

I MET Yossarian for lunch at the Harvest Room[35] in the Nebraska Union. He motioned me to a table to one side of the room.

"Shhhhh!" he said. "They'll see me."

"Who?" I asked, somewhat surprised by Yossarian's sudden secretiveness.

"It's our bitterest rivals," he said, "the infamous Plastic Suit Gang."

"I've never heard of them," I replied. "Which ones are they?"

"Two tables over," he pointed. "See the ones with the blue and red double-knit sportcoats, with white plastic shoes and the name tags that say 'Nebraska Union'?"

"You don't mean the people who run the Union,[36] do you?" I asked.

Yossarian nodded gravely. "They look innocent enough until you watch the things they do."

"Like what? Give me an example," I demanded. "Those men," I said, indignantly, "wear red suits because they're loyal to the University and to the students who eat lunch here every day in their cafeteria."

"Mere camouflage," he responded. "Just analyze your own last statement. Remember, this isn't *their* cafeteria, it's a cafeteria for students."

"But Yossarian, those fellows provide a needed service. Arranging for nonprofit meals every day is no easy task."

"Of course it isn't easy," he exclaimed. "That's why they don't do it!"

"They don't?" I asked.

"Hell no! Do you think those guys care one bit about the thousands of grad students who depend on the Union food service every day?

"Watch them," he instructed. "Here comes one to the cash register now. Listen, does the cashier ask for the full amount?"

"Why, no, she doesn't," I responded. "She's only charging him half price!"

---

[34] *Daily Nebraskan*, 29 October 1975, p. 4.

[35] The Harvest Room, in the student union.

[36] At that time, the "chief" of the Plastic Suit Gang was Daryl Swanson who retired in 2005 after working some four decades on the Lincoln campus in various capacities. Swanson oversaw the dismantling of the professional student union food service in the Harvest Room (and the consequent termination of many longtime university employees) and its replacement by profit-motivated fast food contractors and their poorly-paid workers.

"You see," he said triumphantly. "It's no wonder those guys don't think the prices in the Harvest Room are too high. *They get a 50 per cent discount!*

"And by the way, food service in the Harvest Room is anything but nonprofit. It makes money that the Plastic Suit Gang spends on other 'worthwhile' profit-making schemes, like bowling alleys, pinball machines, and photocopiers."[37]

"That's amazing," I said. "I wouldn't have believed it, taking money from students' food budgets to support other facilities in the Student Union. It's almost criminal when you think about it."

"Lift your feet, Hilligoss," Yossarian commanded. "Here comes the final insult. To remind us that we're *just* students, they send this little man around with a smelly dust mop to sweep under our table and bother us while we're trying to finish our overpriced desserts."

---

[37] The photocopiers actually presented a useful alternative to the dreadful machines offered at that time by the library (see essay 12, below), but, like all facilities in the Union, the machines were operated for profit—a situation always at odds with students' personal budgets.

■ 12 ■

Inferior Photocopies (Inferior copies at 10 cents) [38]

FOLLOWING two weeks of undercover research, Yossarian met me at The Pub[39] and handed me a copy of the Vine Street Irregulars' confidential "Xerox Report." I asked Yossarian why photocopy machines interested the Vine Street Irregulars.

"Many people do not realize it," he said, "but the development of inexpensive, high-quality photocopying has revolutionized the contemporary research scene. This fact is directly relevant to graduate students who are writing seminar papers, theses, and dissertations.

"It is now possible for all graduate students to maintain their own personal libraries of book chapters, research reports, and journal articles. This reduces the time spent in the library, reduces the time previously wasted taking copious notes, and reduces the chance of making misquotes because copies of the original articles are always at hand for ready reference.

"Copying equipment is now an important research aid and, frankly, graduate students at Nebraska work at a disadvantage if efficient, high-quality service is not readily available. The question that interests the Vine Street Irregulars," Yossarian continued, "is why good, inexpensive copying machines are available at many places on campus *but not in the libraries*, where they are most needed?"

I looked at the report, "What did you find out?" I asked.

"First," he said, "Understand that copying services at Nebraska are no small item. For example, the coin-operated machines in the Nebraska Union alone turn out an average of 300,000 copies a year.[40]

---

[38] *Daily Nebraskan*, 12 November 1975, p. 4.

[39] The Pub, 308 South 11th Street.

[40] The Plastic Suit Gang (see essay 11, above) discovered that money could be made by allowing students to use — and thus underwrite — the photocopy machines used in the day-to-day business of the Student Union. At 5-cents per copy, students flocked to use this high-quality machine, and additional machines were soon installed. I remember many evenings when I checked out piles of books from the library and walked to the Union to use the copiers. Curiously, the library staff did not then grasp the notion that the added wear and tear and work of checking books out and back in could be reduced if less expensive copiers were available in the library.

"It's estimated that 500,000 copes are produced each year at Love Memorial Library. At five cents a copy we are talking about $40,000 spent at just the library and the Union."[41]

"I agree that the copy machines in the campus library system leave much to be desired, but do other campus agencies provide good, efficient service?"

"Fortunately, there are," he replied. "First, there are the machines in the Union. And, high-quality, inexpensive copy service is proved by Quick Copy in Burnett Hall at only four cents a copy.[42]

"Reducing copy machines are available at five cents a copy in the Physics Department and at the Lincoln Computing Facility in Nebraska Hall.[43] And ASUN—the Nebraska undergraduate student association—provides copy service at reasonable rates to all student organizations.

"This is not an exhaustive list," he continued, "but it shows that it is possible for many campus agencies to respond to the needs of students, whereas the library has not."

"What's the problem with the library?" I asked.

"It is a complex issue," he said, "but the central question appears to be one of attitude. The library contracts for coin-operated copy services and the machines are maintained by a private company, not by library personnel.

"This is in direct contrast to all other copy services on campus and I think it reflects a deep-seated attitude on the part of the library not to provide high-quality public service in this area.

"Interestingly, the library *does* maintain high-quality copying equipment *for its own internal use*. True, you can use the library's own machine, but they charge

---

[41] Since the non-profit campus Quick Copy service charged only 4-cents per page, it stands to reason that the 5-cents per page charge levied at the Student Union and Love Library resulted in at least 1-cent per page profit for the latter two outlets. That is, respectively, clear profits of $3,000 for the Platic Suit Gang at the Student Union and $5,000 for the private contractor who owned the machines at the library.

[42] The Quick Copy Center, operated by the campus Printing and Duplicating Department, has since moved to the Student Union were it continues to provide a wide range of high-quality services at reasonable prices, but only during regular weekday, day-time business hours.

[43] The utility of reducing/enlarging capabilities was not lost on students who did graphic work of any kind, such as cartography or ad layouts. Reduction capability also gave improved ability to copy from oversize books and journals and to copy two pages of standard-sized books on a single sheet, thus *halving* the cost of copying a long work.

students 10 cents a copy, an exorbitant price that effectively precludes frequent student use."[44]

"Is there an immediate solution?" I asked.

"Sadly, no. The library just signed a one-year contract on September 1st, renewing its present low-level of service. In the interim, all Nebraska students who are dissatisfied with the service have a responsibility to make their opinions known to the library administration. What we need is a *good* 5-cent copy machine!"[45]

The VSI's quest for high-quality 5-cent photocopy machines was amusingly captured by the *Daily Nebraskan's* staff artist.

---

[44] Further complicating matters, the library's own machine was not open to direct use, orders had to be placed and left with a staff member who made the copies during daytime business hours.

[45] In recent years, the photocopy machines in the library are greatly improved, as is the maintenance of the machines —now provided directly by library staff members. The computer revolution now has the Nebraska library system in its expensive and inexorable grip. Future generations of grad students must remain alert to insure that the requisite, up-to-date technological adjuncts to good library research (such as high-tech V-book scanners) are readily and widely available.

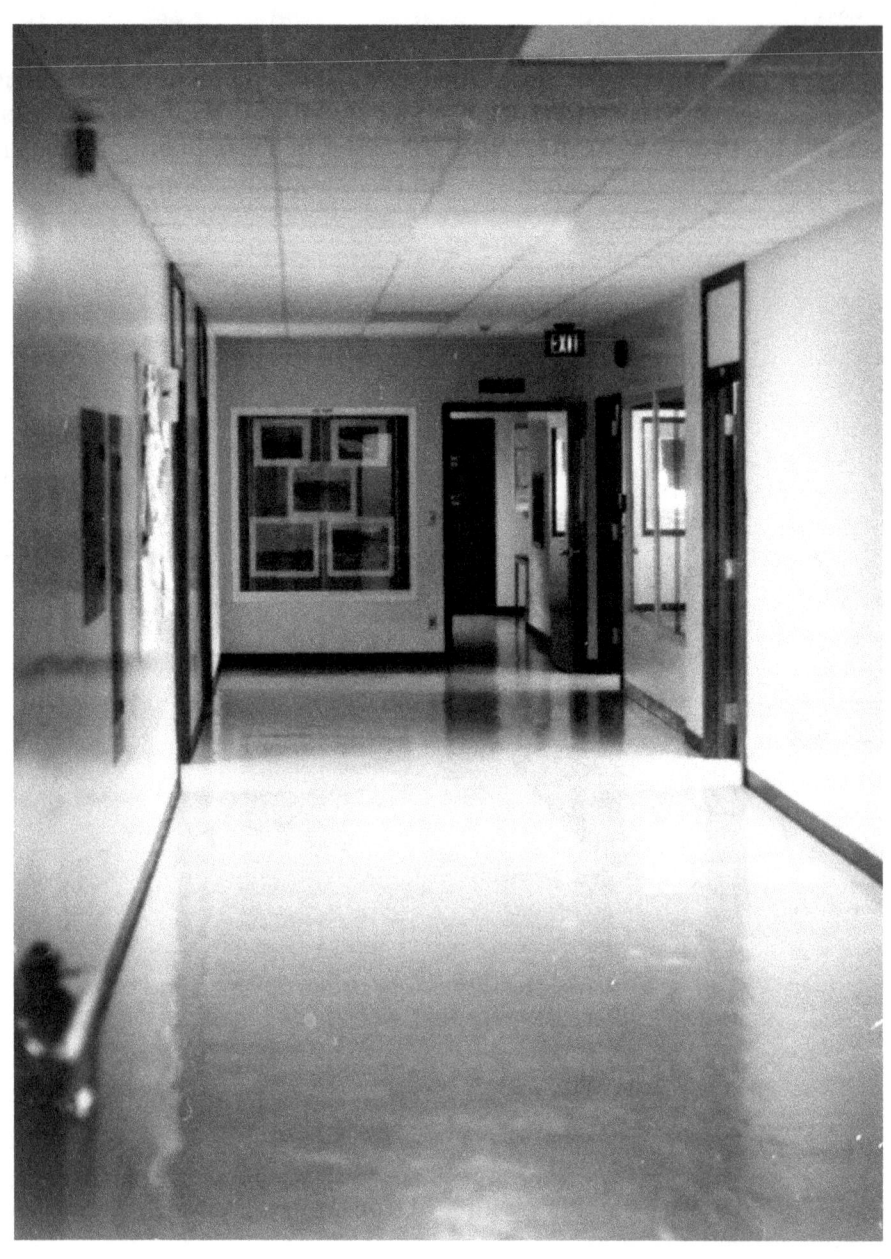

Former entrance to the Department of Geography in Avery Hall
where the "Vine Street Irregulars" dispatches
to the *Daily Nebraskan* were written.

■ 13 ■

Campus as Symbol (Sidewalks are serious talk) [46]

"YOU look a little tight, Yossarian," I observed, noting that he was on his sixth beer.

"I suppose so," he said, "I wrote my comps[47] this week."

"Well then," I said, "I imagine that you're in no mood to discuss the academic aspects of graduate student life."

"Oh, so true! I'd much rather forget about all that business for a little while. How about something more serious?" he proposed.

"*More* serious?" I asked.

"Why, *yes*," he said. "Let's talk about the recent incident of sidewalk defacement reported in the *Daily Nebraskan* last week.[48] Did you read the Campus Police Captain's harsh condemnation of those mischievous students?"

"You can't condone the wanton destruction of University property, can you?" I replied.

"It depends," he said. "Writing in wet cement seems to me a special exception. Perhaps the students' creative energies ought to be lauded — rather than discouraged — by Campus Police.

"Besides, you know," he said, "some social scientists hypothesize that humans incorporate their basic societal values into their built environments. What we witnessed in those students who decorated the sidewalk is a threat to the values of rigidity and order that are symbolized in smooth, clean sidewalks. They didn't materially hurt anything, but they challenged the University on a symbolic level."

"That's quite a thesis," I said, counting Yossarian's seventh beer.

---

[46] *Daily Nebraskan*, 19 November 1975, p. 4.

[47] That is, comprehensive examinations; the form, format, duration, consistency, scheduling, administration, grading and content of these exams varied considerably, sometimes seemingly perversely, by department and discipline. At the M.A. level, comps were typically graded anonymously; thus, a professor could give an "A" to a student in his or her course while anonymously flunking the student on a departmentally-administered comp. This provided a mechanism for getting rid of otherwise competent students that given professors simply "didn't like" for various reasons. By contrast, Ph.D. comps, administered by each student's doctoral supervisory committee, provide no anonymity to the graders. At the doctoral level, if enough professors want to get rid of a student, they simply band together and refuse to form a supervisory committee in the first place, an action for which the hapless student, having completed all of his or her coursework, has no recourse.

[48] "Vandals hit new cement," *Daily Nebraskan*, 14 November 1975, p. 1.

"Oh, it doesn't stop there," he continued. "Consider Oldfather Hall.[49] The Dean's office is at the top and the students' lounge[50] is at the bottom. What does that tell you about the order of things?

"And look how most of the academic departments are partitioned off in their own little physical preserves. That tells you that we value ease of administration above ease of interdisciplinary communication."

"Try the Big Red stadium,"[51] I prompted, realizing that there was no stopping him now.

"Sure," he said, taking up the challenge. "How revealing of Nebraska values that the largest physical structure on campus is dedicated to football instead of academic education. But that's enough for now. Let's go on over to Casey's.[52] I want you to meet some friends of mine."

As we left the Town Tavern,[53] I couldn't help thinking Yossarian must have been disappointed that someone didn't ask him to discuss the social symbolism of architecture on a comp question. Perhaps next week he'll be back in his old frame of mind.

---

[49] At twelve stories, Oldfather Hall resembles an upended shoebox. In the ultimate symbolic act, Hardy Jones, a professor in the department of Philosophy, committed suicide by jumping from the window of his 10th-floor office (*Lincoln Star Journal*, 1 November 1983, p. 6).

[50] The student lounge was really more of a bare bones canteen, replete with coin-operated vending machines for soda pop, coffee, and snacks. Until the Arts and Sciences Dean subsequently banned smoking in the lounge it became a hangout for a noticeably thuggish and aggressively territorial stripe of student.

[51] According to oft-repeated Huskerland bravado, Memorial Stadium becomes the 3rd largest "city" in Nebraska on football weekends.

[52] Casey's Beverage, 1020 "P" Street.

[53] The Town Tavern, 1115 "P" Street.

Censure the President of the Faculty Senate (Eldridge skirts grad issues) [54]

WHEN I returned home last night a brown envelope was under the door. I suspected I had been visited by Yossarian.

Opening the envelope, I found a secret Vine Street Irregulars report titled: "Analysis of the Eldridge Manifesto."[55] Due to the timely nature of the document, I think I should make it public immediately:

(1) Although Franklin Eldridge would have people believe otherwise, our concern over his so-called "explanatory" statement about classes not being met by graduate assistants avoids the main issue. The main issue is his unfounded allegation of graduate assistant irresponsibility. Eldridge should not be permitted to skirt this issue.

(2) Eldridge is unable to support his allegations. His assertions are based primarily on his experiences as Associate Dean of the College of Agriculture.[56] He neither details the facts and figures of that experience nor justifies why his experience in that one college can be considered representative of graduate assistants in other colleges.

(3) Eldridge's allegations cannot be supported on the basis of his present position in the Department of Animal Science. Vine Street Irregulars confirm that his department has only *one* graduate teaching assistant.

(4) The only "facts" Eldridge actually marshals are, presumably, from the files of the campus Ombudsman's office. At most, these files reveal only *two* cases of graduate assistants not meeting their classes. Nonetheless, Eldridge claims that

---

[54] *Daily Nebraskan*, 3 December 1975, p. 4.

[55] Franklin E. Eldridge (1918–2017) was a professor of animal science and president of the UNL Faculty Senate. He stated, for example, "It's the first year assistants or the graduate assistants who haven't learned what the world of work is like who don't meet their classes" *(Daily Nebraskan*, 12 November 1975, p. 3). He urged the Faculty Senate to take action. In response, the Graduate Student Association unanimously rejected Eldridge's assertion (see letter from Cassie Hergenrader, *Daily Nebraskan*, 19 November 1975, p. 4). Eldridge's lame defense appeared in the *Daily Nebraskan* (24 November 1975, p. 4).

[56] College of Agriculture, now named the Institute of Agriculture and Natural Resources (IANR). Students and administrators on the "East Campus" (or "Ag Campus" anywhere else), have traditionally been more conservative. Eldridge had little experience or familiarity with the graduate students on the main or "City" campus where the traditional arts and sciences programs are housed.

this number is seriously out of proportion to the number of classes taught by graduate assistants. Vine Street Irregulars report that there are 598 teaching assistants at Nebraska and conclude that only two complaints—in who knows how many years—is a favorable record.

Further, after considerable investigation, the Vine Street Irregulars report they are unable to discover the specific number of classes for which graduate assistants are solely responsible. Thus, Eldridge's claimed ability to gather such information on such short notice is seriously questioned.

(5) Eldridge's method of inference deserves further investigation. The Vine Street Irregulars are unable to find any statisticians who would make inferences based on a sample of six, as did Eldridge. Further, the Irregulars are unable to find any statistical test which permits frequencies of only one or two in each cell, as required for Eldridge's "analysis." (Snedecor, the agricultural statistician, must be red with shame. Irregulars on the East Campus are instructed to apologize to Snedecor on behalf of all grad students at Nebraska).[57]

(6) Given that Eldridge's amazing statistical test can actually be produced, he must also be required to state the level of statistical significance he finds personally acceptable. This will indicate the degree of his readiness to accept or reject unfounded inferences.

(7) Eldridge concludes: "It is unfortunate that irresponsibility on the part of a very limited number of persons casts aspersions on the great majority of responsible persons." The Vine Street Irregulars High Command wholeheartedly agrees that "the great majority" are indeed "responsible persons." It *is, however,* unfortunate that the irresponsible and unfounded assertions of the president of the Faculty Senate casts doubt on the manner of man that the faculty find acceptable as their official spokesman. The Vine Street Irregulars High Command encourages the Faculty Senate to either censure their president or remove him from office.

(8) The Vine Street Irregulars must not forget that Eldridge's remarks comprise much more than "hot air" expounded in a local bar. His irresponsible words were published in media where members of the Nebraska Legislature could read them. Eldridge acted as the spokesman of the faculty senate. He holds a position of trust and responsibility and has abused that position. Eldridge's admission that the emphasis he placed on graduate assistants was "probably stronger than should have been made" wins the Vine Street Irregulars award for most cowardly understatement of the year. The Vine Street Irregulars demand a full retraction, published in the public media.

---

[57] George W. Snedecor (1881–1974) was a fixture at Iowa State University and the author of *Statistical Methods Applied to Experiments in Agriculture and Biology*, a standard, oft-revised text since 1937, one with which Eldridge should have been familiar.

■ 15 ■

Putting Grad Skills to Work (VSI increases grad identity)[58]

YOSSARIAN dropped by Friday evening at my invitation to help open a new case of wine. He settled down, glass in hand.

"To the VSI!" he toasted.

"To graduate students everywhere!" I joined in.

"Yossarian," I said, "this may be a good time to sit back and reflect on the accomplishments of the semester and your plans for next year."

"Yes," he agreed. "In reviewing VSI accomplishments, I would stress an increased identity for graduate students at UNL.

"Many grads have found that they share the concerns of the VSI. All that had to be done was make these concerns public where they could be discussed, evaluated and acted upon.

"We now see the increased activity of the Graduate Student Association," Yossarian continued. "We see active participation of graduate students in ASUN. We see more letters to the editor in the *Daily Nebraskan* that are signed by graduate students. This signifies an increased level of awareness.

"Where it will go from here is an open question," he said.

"There has also been a corresponding awakening of the university community to the existence of graduate students. One hears the VSI quoted at the administrative level of the university. I hope this awareness will increase in time and spread to groups such as the Regents and the Alumni Association. This is one future job for the VSI."

I interrupted to ask if the VSI has any specific plans next year.

Yossarian responded, "There are several things we are thinking about. Here are some examples:

(1) Ask grad students in business and economics to complete a detailed audit and analysis of Nebraska Union internal budgets.

(2) Request philosophy grad students to help re-evaluate the traditional ethics of the university community toward the uses and accumulation of knowledge.

(3) Ask our fellows in the Law College to complete an examination of the legal status of graduate students, relating to free speech in classrooms, tenure as teaching assistants and the graduate catalog as a legal contract.

(4) Request grad students in sociology to examine the possibility of grads unionizing and/or affiliating with AAUP as student members.

---

[58] *Daily Nebraskan*, 10 December 1975, p. 4.

(5) Request social work grad students to undertake a new look at the graduate student as a disadvantaged minority."

"Hold it!" I said. "I think I get the picture. You advocate the use of specialized grad student skills to help identify, articulate and propose solutions to problems related to the quality of graduate student life and education."

"Exactly," he said. "I hope that during Christmas break grad students will think about how they can contribute, singly or in groups, to the continuing efforts of the VSI to make graduate student life at UNL a more rewarding experience.

"There is no limit to the topics which might be covered in theses, dissertations and seminar papers relating to the general problems of graduate education. Everyone is encouraged to put their own special talents to work.

"What a Christmas present that would be for the VSI!"

■ 16 ■

Welcome Back (Where's Rosemary Woods when we need a tape gap?) [59]

YOSSARIAN'S face still radiated the warm, relaxed glow of Christmas cheer and an apparently convivial New Year's Eve party.

"Hilligoss," he said, hoisting a mug of beer at Duffy's,[60] "it was good to get away from academia for a while."

"Well," I replied, "it looks to me like you certainly took advantage of the opportunity."

"True!" he said, nodding sheepishly in agreement. "But now I'm rested up for another semester in Lincolnland. Imagine, four more months of escape from the 'real world' of work, as some call it, are here at hand. What a joy to be an overworked, underpaid graduate student . . . ."

"Yossarian," I interrupted, "I know you didn't have me come all this way just to sing the praises of graduate student life. Do you have something from the Vine Street Irregulars that might interest my readers?" I asked, noting the small, brown package in his hands.

"Oh, yes!" he said, "I almost forgot. I have a tape. The quality isn't very good, but we think it's a welcoming speech given last week by a department Chair to his returning graduate students. We aren't sure where it came from, but we thought you'd be interested."

"Thanks," I said. After Yossarian left, I listened to the tape. Here is a transcript (with names deleted):

SPEAKER (older male): "It's good to see you again and I trust you are all looking forward to a productive and stimulating semester. I do, however, want to comment on the rumor that some of you were not pleased with the program here last semester. Several points need to be covered:

"First, there is simply no truth to the rumor that Professor _____ was poorly prepared for his course. I have spoken with the Professor and he assures me that the visiting high school student who demolished his thesis during the proseminar must have been a child genius possessing incredible intellectual gifts as well as very bad manners.

---

[59] *Daily Nebraskan*, 16 January 1976, p. 4.

[60] Duffy's Tavern, 1412 "O" Street, site of numerous foosball and table shuffleboard contests.

"Second, be assured that the ban on grad student use of departmental pencils is not intended as a slight to graduate teaching assistants. I assure you that the deficit in K-budget funds was necessitated by the pressing need to provide Professor _____ with unlimited Xeroxing for his research work. The fact that his article was subsequently rejected simply illustrates that we need more funds. As graduate students, you must realize that finances are the key to good research and that we want our faculty to have every possible advantage. This is why we must also impose a ban on grad student use of departmental paper clips this semester.[61]

"Finally, I do not want you to worry unduly about the students who dropped out at the end of last semester. There is no veracity in the rumor that we, as a faculty, were unhappy with their contributions to the intellectual and social atmosphere of the department.[62] We will, however, sorely miss the income from the National Science Foundation research fellowships that the three students in question took with them to another campus.[63]

"So, as you can see, any basis for dissatisfaction on your part is completely unwarranted. I hope this clears the air such that we can now get down to work. If there are any problems you would like to discuss further, please arrange to see me during the special office hour I have reserved for graduate students, 9:30 a.m. to 10:00 a.m. every third Tuesday of the month." END OF TRANSCRIPT

I thought to myself, "this tape must be something from the improvisation lab in the drama department. I couldn't be real, or could it?"

---

[61] Not an exaggeration. It was so bad in one department that when junior *faculty* members asked for paper clips the secretaries would respond with, "How many?" and then count out the requested number of clips, one by one.

[62] Students frequently "disappeared" without explanation from programs in many departments, often due to enforcement of unofficial rules regarding behavior and deportment. In one case, a student received a severe tongue lashing for playing solitaire at his desk late one afternoon; a female TA was upbraided for not wearing a skirt when she taught; and another student was severely reprimanded for not erasing the blackboard after making a seminar presentation. Students were routinely flunked out of programs for failing to study texts that never appeared on any official reading list. The often capricious nature of faculty evaluations of graduate student behavior and performance remains an enduring problem in graduate education today, and occurs in ever more subtle and pernicious new forms.

[63] The provision that at least some externally-funded graduate student grants could be transferred to other institutions was treated as "secret knowledge" by the faculty in most departments. Many students of my acquaintance would have made very different choices in their graduate training if they had realized that their external grants and fellowships were, in some cases, transferrable to other schools.

■ 17 ■

Meeting Leonik (Fainthearted dissension; make ripples, not waves) [64]

I ANSWERED the door to my apartment to find Yossarian in the company of another graduate student whose name, I learned, was "Leonik."[65] Yossarian was in good spirits and he considered this meeting to be a special event. It was the first time I had actually met face-to-face with a member of the Vine Street Irregulars' High Command and Yossarian furnished a bottle with which to commemorate my acceptance into Leonik's confidence.

Leonik, as you will discover from our ensuing conversation, is the Vine Street Irregulars' official ideologist. Yossarian nursed his drink alone in the living room while Leonik and I talked over coffees at the small table in my tiny kitchen.

"I understand, Hilligoss, that Yossarian trusts you explicitly," said Leonik, as he lowered the blinds and drew the curtains together. "I must trust you to never reveal my identity to your readers. To do so would undoubtedly jeopardize my graduate career."

I assured him that I would hold his identity in confidence, but thought to myself that his case of paranoia seemed overly developed. I learned later, however, that his bewhiskered head was filled with radical, sometimes revolutionary, ideas.

"Leonik," I began, "What is the current mood of graduate students at the University of Nebraska?"

"There are no blazing issues within the ranks of Nebraska graduate students, only the smolderings of discontent and cynicism," he said, fingering his coffee cup. "We grumble and complain among ourselves but we do not effectively carry our case to the administration, the Nebraska Legislature, or the people of Nebraska. But far worse," he said, "we have lost hold of our moral fiber. We often tell ourselves that it is best not to make waves or cause a fuss, but in doing so we lose all claims to intellectual integrity. Many of us have become cynical and distrustful of academia and yet many of us want to become teachers.

"We tell ourselves that things can't be so bad in other schools and that eventually we will leave Nebraska behind. But is this the case? Shouldn't we ask ourselves where the administrators at Nebraska came from before they got here?

---

[64] *Daily Nebraskan*, 23 January 1976, p. 4.

[65] The origin of the name "Leonik" now escapes me. I think it just sounded quaintly "subversive," so I used it.

What makes us think we will leave poor administration and academic politics behind when we depart Nebraska to become instructors in other schools?

"We imagine that things must be different elsewhere," Leonik continued, "because it excuses us from our responsibilities right here in Nebraska. We should realize that, for those of us in graduate school, Nebraska is not the end of the world. It is our beginning. This is the time and the place to profess the things we know to be right. If we can't start here, where can we? But which one of us is ready to commit the crimes of Galileo? There are too few, Hilligoss, that is the sad thing—and that is what characterizes the mood of graduate students at Nebraska."

We sat in silence, finishing our coffee. I thanked Leonik for his visit and we joined Yossarian in the living room.

"Time for another drink," Yossarian suggested. Leonik nodded assent but his heart wasn't in it. I thought again about Leonik's display of paranoia. Was he really afraid of the administration, or was he more concerned about keeping the few graduate student friends as he had in his own department—"friends" who had already started to "play the game"?[66]

---

[66] The disillusionment that comes from being "sold out" by a fellow graduate student is the most cruel of all. One expects it sometimes from faculty and administrators, but not from one's student colleagues.

■ 18 ■

Coffee Economics (Student Union's coffee not worth its cream and sugar)[67]

LEONIK rattled his empty coffee cup noisily on our corner table in the Harvest Room at the Nebraska Union.

"Hilligoss, do you realize that a second cup of coffee here is going to cost me just as much as the first?" he asked, visibly irritated.

"I agree," I said "it is a little annoying to have to pay full price every time you get a refill."

"It's not just a matter of inconvenience," Leonik pressed, "the whole Union set-up is indicative of the Union management's failure to understand and meet the common, everyday needs of the majority of students at the University of Nebraska."

"The matter of free refills for a cup of coffee is minor, but it serves to illustrate my point," he continued. "The Union management obviously does not realize that *any good intellectual discussion worth its cream and sugar will last through at least two cups of coffee!* The same is true for a good novel, essay, or proper preparation of a class assignment. One cup of coffee just won't do it."

Leonik handed me a brown paper envelope, it looked like another Vine Street Irregulars report.

"What's this?" I said, opening it carefully.

"Take a look," said Leonik, "it's the Vine Street Irregulars' secret report on the cost of two cups of coffee. Undercover agents visited 13 local establishments that serve coffee and recorded the total cost of two cups of coffee, tax included."

The information read as follows:

---

[67] *Daily Nebraskan*, 30 January 1976, p. 4.

THE VSI TWO-CUP COFFEE PRICE REPORT

Establishment [68]	1st cup	2nd cup	Total Cost
Dippy Donuts	21 cents	21 cents	42 cents
UNL HARVEST ROOM	**16 cents**	**16 cents**	**32 cents**
Hilton Hotel	31 cents	free	31 cents
Barrymore's	26 cents	free	26 cents
Hansen's Place	16 cents	10 cents	26 cents
International House of Pancakes	26 cents	free	26 cents
Scott's Pancake Shoppe	26 cents	free	26 cents
Burger Chef	21 cents	free	21 cents
Kuhl's Restaurant	21 cents	free	21 cents
Oscar's	21 cents	free	21 cents
Super Sub	21 cents	free	21 cents
Terminal Drug	21 cents	free	21 cents
Mr. "B" Kountry Kitchen	10 cents	10 cents	20 cents

"You will note," observed Leonik, "that the Harvest Room in the Nebraska Union was found to be the second most expensive place to have *two* cups of coffee. It was exceeded in cost only by an establishment which: (a) provides 24-hour service, (b) provides waiter/waitress service, (c) depends on the sale of coffee and donuts for its sole income, and (d) is powered (quite properly) by the profit motive."

"But," I interrupted, "the cost of *one* cup of coffee is quite a bit lower in the Union. In fact, it's almost the lowest."

"Exactly," responded Leonik. "*One* cup of coffee is just enough for the fifteen minute coffee breaks taken by the Union's management and staff!"

I looked down at my empty coffee cup. "I'll buy, I could use another."

"No thanks," said Leonik. "Let's go downtown for that second cup. Besides, I've just moved my checking account off campus and I need to go visit my new bank; unlike the one in the student Union, it offers free checking."

---

[68] Dippy Donuts, 1227 "R" Street; Hilton Hotel, 141 North 9th Street; Barrymore's, 124 North 13th Street; Henry's Place, 1123 "R" Street; International House of Pancakes, 1435 "Q" Street; Scott's Pancake Shoppe, 401 South 13th Street; Burger Chef, 13th and "P" Streets; Kuhl's Restaurant, 1038 "O" Street; Oscar's Lounge, 245 N. 13th Street; Super Sub, 215 North 14th Street; Terminal Drug, 947 "O" Street; Mr. "B" Kountry Kitchen, 1010 "N" Street.

■ 19 ■

Clear the Decks! (Choice of new chancellor warning to duff draggers)[69]

LEONIK motioned me to a booth in a darkened alcove in Brannigan's Restaurant.[70] In our scruffy, grad student attire,[71] we sat down under the reproachful gaze of two giddy but apparently pleasant blondes who were obviously out for a sophisticated night on the town. Socialization wasn't on Leonik's agenda.

"Two coffees," ordered Leonik. "Now, Hilligoss," he said, "I have work for you."

"Wait a minute, I'm not a Vine Street Irregular!" I replied.

"Don't interrupt!" Leonik cut in. "Do you recognize this man?" he said, pushing a faded photograph under my nose.

"I guess so," I said, thinking it looked like the Dean of the Graduate College.

"We've got to get to him," said Leonik. "It must be done."

"Hey, look," I said, "I'm an undergraduate columnist, not a hit man."

"That's just the point," replied Leonik. "We don't want you to do him any harm. We just want you to get a message to him. The Dean's a nice guy, after all, but he's not on the Chancellor search committee. He's not privy to the latest news, the search committee is sworn to secrecy."

"I don't understand" I said.

"Look, it won't do him any good with the Regents to be seen talking to an Irregular, but we think he ought to be told that they're just about ready to pick a new Chancellor for the University of Nebraska. You can tell him, or write a column."

"But everybody knows we're choosing a new Chancellor," I said.

Leonik retorted, "In general, yes, but one of the *specific* candidates they're thinking about is deeply concerned about the low amount of graduate research grant money the University attracts each year! If he's selected as Chancellor, it means a lot of folks will have to get off their collective duffs and get to work writing grant

---

[69] *Daily Nebraskan*, 13 February 1976, p. 4.

[70] Brannigan's Restaurant, 1228 "P" Street.

[71] My basic wardrobe at the time consisted of one "good" suit from my high school years, several pairs of jeans, a few dress shirts, and four long-wearing and surprisingly presentable Harris tweed jackets (purchased for $1.25 each at the Salvation Army thrift store). In subsequent years, I assembled a sizeable collection of Giorgio Armani neckties for $1 (or less) each from cast-offs donated to thrift stores by Lincoln's well-heeled attorneys (it's a collection I still treasure).

applications—and that would mean a flurry of extra work for the Graduate College. The Irregulars think that our one man in the administration ought to be prepared for all the activity—so he can clear the decks."

"O.K.," I said, "I suppose you've got some suggestions on how to get things under way?"

"Of course," he said. "We have a few ideas to open the lines of communication, and help every department look more impressive to potential funders.

"First, we need a full-time Graduate College Advocate. This person, unlike an ombudsman, would seek out trouble spots, review specific departmental policies, and generally see to it that each department gets the help it needs to keep its graduate program in the best possible health.

"Second, we need a Student Advisory Board for the Graduate College, modeled on the undergraduate version that now exists in the College of Arts and Sciences. This would help keep the Graduate College directly informed about graduate student needs. In fact, it would be a great idea if each college, especially Arts and Sciences, established a *Graduate Student* Advisory Board. This would demonstrate creative administrative leadership—and educational foundations would love it!

"Finally, we need a little comradeship and *esprit de corps* among the members of all the graduate programs. How about some convocations, sponsored by the Graduate College, that speak directly to the goals and future directions of graduate education at Nebraska?"

"Think of it," said Leonik, a tough new Chancellor and our Graduate College Dean *working together* to improve graduate research funding[72] at Nebraska. I hope the system President and the Regents make the right choice."

---

[72] With time and experience, I have become far less sanguine about accepting money from external agencies, especially when there are strings attached. The aim of money-raising efforts in colleges and universities must be to advance the specific interests and self-generated projects of the faculty members and/or students directly affected, never to advance the goals promulgated by the funding sources. It's much better to be impoverished and creative than to spend one's time as a contract laborer doing work in which you have no intellectual interest.

■ 20 ■

Lessons from the Faculty Union Vote (Union vote analysis helps VSI design grad strategy) [73]

I JOINED my contacts at a large table in the Nebraska Union's Harvest Room. Yossarian, for once, appeared sober. I can't help but think that Leonik is a good influence on him; but I hope that making Yossarian wear a T-shirt proclaiming: "Coffee Drinkers Are Better Lovers!" isn't pushing a bit too hard. Leonik surreptitiously poured a round of "illegal" coffee refills from his Thermos.

"What's the word?" I asked.

"Cream and sugar," mumbled Yossarian, under his breath, helping himself to the Union's condiments.

"The faculty vote," said Leonik.

"The vote on collective bargaining?" I asked. Does that interest the Vine Street Irregulars?"

"We've been watching the move toward faculty unionization for some time," he replied. "We think we might pick up some tips on what *not* to do when we finally get enough strength to press for the unionization of graduate teaching assistants."

"Well," I asked, "did you learn something?"

"We've just a preliminary analysis," said Leonik, "but you're welcome to see it." From one of Leonik's ubiquitous brown envelopes, he exhumed a freshly-typed report and handed it to me. It read:

THE FACULTY UNION VOTE—VSI ANALYSIS

(1) The recent loss on the unionization vote was not felt by the professors to be a serious blow.[74] A faculty with an 80 per cent tenure level already has a union in almost everything but name. Lesson: A future move toward unionization will be more risky for TAs than for the faculty. We don't have tenure to fall back on when we speak out against "the management."

---

[73] *Daily Nebraskan*, 20 February 1976, p. 4.

[74] "Faculty vote defeats union," *Daily Nebraskan*, February 18, 1976, p. 1. At the same time professors' salaries were very low; see "Full professor salaries at NU rank at bottom of AAU barrel," *Daily Nebraskan*, March 3, 1976, p. 1 An activist faction within the faculty tried again for unionization in 1984. I was one of two graduate students hired during that campaign by the American Association of University Professors to assist in the unionization effort, so I had a front row seat. The effort failed for many of the same reasons as before (*Daily Nebraskan*, April 16, 1984, pp. 1-2).

(2) Large blocks of faculty members apparently broke ranks under political pressure from the system-level administration. The general absence of signatures from the Institute of Agricultural and Natural Resources[75] (horticulture excepted) on the Open Letter endorsing collective bargaining in last Friday's *Daily Nebraskan* was conspicuous.[76] Lesson: Large blocks of potential resistance resulting from conservative forces and thinly-veiled threats made by reactionary deans and department chairs must be identified and dealt with well in advance.

(3) Major numerical support for faculty unionization was concentrated in only a few departments. The English Department alone accounted for over 28 percent of the signatures on the Open Letter. Ten departments (all but one in the College of Arts and Sciences) accounted for over 70 per cent of all the signatures. Lesson: Don't move for unionization of TAs until a campus-wide base of support has actually been assembled.

(4) Faculty leadership was spotty. Only five departments had more that 50 percent signature participation on the Open Letter (i.e., Political Science 78 per cent, Sociology 76 per cent, Classics 75 percent, Horticulture 63 percent, and Psychology 55 per cent). Lesson: Cultivate effective leadership within as many departments as possible.

(5) The faculty did not include TAs in the proposed bargaining plans. Lesson: Graduate students must look out for their own interests. Faculty members do not treat us as colleagues when power and money are at stake.

"I gather," I mused, "this isn't the best time for the Irregulars to demand unionization for grad students?"

"You've got that right," Leonik answered. "Let's go to Kuhl's[77] for some coffee — my thermos is empty."

---

[75] IANR, formerly the College of Agriculture. Strategically, the unfortunate inclusion of the State's numerous Agricultural Extension Agents—they enjoyed faculty appointments in IANR even though they rarely, if ever, taught classes—in the collective bargaining vote introduced a conservative bloc that the more liberal City Campus factions could not overcome.

[76] "To Our Faculty Colleagues," *Daily Nebraskan*, February 13, 1976, p. 10. The letter bore 198 signatures. Since the balloting was secret, the Open Letter was the only available empirical measure of support for unionization. It is a flawed and imperfect measure, but the signatures of those willing to stand up and be counted provided the only glimpse into the attitudes of the faculty as a whole.

[77] Kuhl's Restaurant, 1038 "O" Street. Kuhl's Restaurant plied many students with wholesome—if sometimes somewhat bland—meals. The daily noon special was served until 4:00 p.m., enabling a late lunch to double as an economical early dinner. Breakfast at Kuhl's provided a look—and a listen—into the world of downtown businessmen (they were all males) who convened everyday at "their" table for coffee, gossip and political intrigue.

■ 21 ■

Bereuter's Scapegoats (TA's are bracing themselves for blitzkrieg)[78]

"HILLIGOSS," Leonik began, "there are several items in which your readers should take some interest. The Vine Street Irregulars anticipate an imminent attack on graduate teaching assistants."

"Really?" I said. "What are the warning signs?"

"Three things," responded Leonik. "First, there is the Regents' plan to review the quality of undergraduate education at the University of Nebraska. Second, there are the recent comments of State Senator Douglas Bereuter[79] (a former professor at Nebraska) that the quality of undergraduate teaching at Nebraska is undermined partially by the extensive use of graduate teaching assistants.[80] And, finally, there is the faculty work-load survey now in progress."

"What's the connection" I asked.

Leonik took a deep breath. "First," he said, "the work-load survey will undoubtedly show that in several departments graduate teaching assistants are carrying as much as *50 per cent* of the teaching contact hours with undergraduates. This finding will confirm Bereuter's suspicion that too much undergraduate teaching is conducted by TAs. And finally, the Regents will have a new scapegoat, the graduate teaching assistant."

"Pretty amazing," I said.

"Yes, it is," he agreed. "It's amazing because there are several points that will be skipped during the administrative and legislative analyses of the situation. For example, with TAs doing so much of the teaching, will anyone ask what the

---

[78] *Daily Nebraskan*, 27 February 1976, p. 4.

[79] Douglas K. Bereuter was an urban planner turned Republican politician. He served in the Nebraska Legislature from 1975 to 1979 and was elected to the U.S. House of Representatives in 1978; he was re-elected 12 times.

[80] Aspects of Bereuter's criticisms had some merit. It was my experience, for example, that undergraduate education at the then Municipal University of Omaha—where, for example, all geography courses, including labs, were taught by tenured or tenure-track professors—was vastly superior to undergraduate education generally at the University of Nebraska-Lincoln where many introductory-level courses were taught by TAs, or by professors in large, anonymous classes of 200 to 300 students. At the same time, however, courses taught by mature, highly motivated, advanced graduate students at Nebraska could be superior to those offered by the more egregious examples of tenured deadwood. Bereuter's mistake lay in failing to understand such distinctions.

regular faculty members are doing with their time? And, assuming that the regular faculty members aren't goofing off, will the Nebraska Legislature be willing to foot the cost of putting a Ph.D. in front of every classroom? And, most important, will anyone really ask why the teaching done by TAs is considered *inherently* inferior to that of full-time doctorates? Will anyone expose such a conclusion as the *assumption* that it is? Obviously, many TAs are superior teachers compared to many tenured profs, *and vice versa*. Why blame *only* the TAs?"

"What can I do?" I asked.

"If you can," said Leonik, "try to get the following points across to Bereuter in one of your columns." I summarize Leonik's case as follows:

(1) TAs are frequently the most enthusiastic, up-to-date teachers that many undergraduates will ever encounter. Most TAs have a sense of idealism and love for learning not yet dulled by the difficulties of teaching at Nebraska for twenty years or more.

(2) The TAs who have full-course responsibility (rather than minor roles in lab or discussion sections) almost always have recent master's degrees and are about as "up" on recent developments in their discipline as anyone needs to be to teach introductory undergraduate courses.

(3) If it really is the case that TAs aren't qualified to teach, then Bereuter's time would be better spent investigating the quality of *graduate education* at Nebraska. He should note the paradox that the full-time professors he wants to do more undergraduate teaching are the *same* professors who are training the TAs that he finds objectionable!

(4) Bereuter may not realize that Nebraska can't always attract the best graduate TAs simply because of administrative red-tape. Several departments do not receive authorization from the administration to make firm financial offers to prospective TAs until July or August of each year.[81] By then, many of the most capable TAs have already accepted positions at other universities. Now that, Senator Bereuter, is a *real* problem that needs to be solved.

"OK," I said, "I'll write the column, but I can't guarantee Bereuter will read it."

"All you can do is try," said Leonik. "How about a cup of coffee at Henry's?"[82]

---

[81] At the time, this problem was especially acute in the Department of Modern Languages — wherein several grad students sat on pins and needles all summer long before learning whether their assistantships had been renewed for the fall. This was a brutal and unconscionable practice.

[82] Henry's Place, 1123 "R" Street, a campus landmark for many years, on the site of the present Lied Center, frequented by music and art students and faculties. Henry's was a "classic" college restaurant from the 1940s, replete with rows of white wooden booths, university memorabilia on the walls, "daily specials," and huge cinnamon rolls.

■ 22 ■

The Job Market (M.A. degrees could become present-day scarlet letters) [83]

I ANSWERED the telephone and heard Leonik's voice saying, "Is that you Hilligoss? I'm in Omaha and we've got a problem on our hands."

"What is it?" I asked, fearing the worst.

"It's Yossarian," he said, "it's just awful."

"Yossarian?" I aksed, "what's wrong?"

"Oh, how to explain it? We're at the Dundee Dell[84] on Dodge Street and Yossarian's drunk out of his mind. I can't bring him back on the bus like this. I hate to impose, but could you drive to Omaha and pick us up?"

I agreed to become their chauffeur, and I also began to wonder what could have happened to push Yossarian to so exceed his usually amazing tolerance for alcohol.

After we returned to Lincoln and Yossarian was delivered safely to his apartment, Leonik told me the whole story. Yossarian, now that he had completed his master's degree, can't find a job.

"No job at all?" I asked. My tone betrayed my disbelief.

"That's right," Leonik confirmed. "He met today with a personnel representative from the company that was his last hope."

"Surely he can get a temporary job in the meantime," I said, trying to be reassuring.

"You'd think so!" exclaimed Leonik. "But that's a dead-end too. As soon as you apply for a job for which you're overqualified, if anything, just to tide you through, they tell you: we'd like to hire you but we can't afford to pay you what you deserve, and then they turn around and give the job to some twerp with a C+ average and B.A. degree! Some employers apparently fear that we'll leave as soon as we get the chance, and others are more than a little intimidated by our graduate training. Try getting an entry-level sales job after you tell them you have a Ph.D.! We eggheads are just too threatening to lots of folks outside academia.

"What's to be done," I asked. "The Vine Street Irregulars must have some thoughts on this problem?"

"Yes, there are three things that the University should be doing," said Leonik. I summarize his major points below:

---

[83] *Daily Nebraskan*, 12 March 1976, p. 4.

[84] Dundee Dell tavern, 4969 Dodge Street, Omaha, Nebraska.

(1) The University has a moral responsibility to discourage students who seek graduate education *primarily* as a means to higher income. Conversely, as some professional schools now do, the University should *not* limit graduate enrollments because the job market is saturated. Everyone should be welcomed to pursue as much education as they can handle, so long as it remains first and foremost an adventure of the mind and is not motivated by the raw quest for mammon. Graduate school should never be about making money, it should be about the love of learning.

(2) The University has a responsibility to educate the general public about the real nature of graduate education, to encourage public acceptance of individuals with graduate education in positions not usually recognized as prestige jobs. Why can't a cab driver or an orderly or a letter carrier have a Ph.D.? As a society, we need to seriously rethink the fundamental relationship between work and education, and the University's public relations department could help get the ball rolling, to start a public discussion.

(3) In the short term, a program is needed in which the University actively seeks to match graduate students with sympathetic employers. The administration does this aggressively for undergraduates, but doesn't do nearly enough for graduate students. The folks at the University's placement office look confused, dumbfounded, and put out when you tell them you are a thirty-five year old graduate student—and that you want to find a job.

"Those sound like reasonable options," I observed. "I suppose Yossarian could always join the Army if everything else fails."

"He can't even do that," said an exasperated Leonik. "He's too old. His thirtieth birthday is two weeks from today!"[85]

---

[85] The maximum ages at which a person can enlist in the U.S. military varies by service branch, prior service, specialties, and other considerations. "Yossarian might well have found a way in, but he was nearing the upper age limits. The U.S. Air Force had an upper ceiling of 27 years of age whereas other branches were more flexible.

■ 23 ■

Real Politics (Only 'real politics' can change rhetoric) [86]

I CROSSED paths with Leonik as he came out of The Mill[87] with an armload of coffee beans. "Hilligoss!" he greeted me. "Come on down to Scott's Pancake Shoppe[88] and we'll have a cup of coffee together."

"Certainly," I agreed. "Tell me," I asked, "are you satisfied with the outcome of the ASUN elections?

"Can't say that I followed the campaign with much enthusiasm," he replied.

"But there were graduate students running of office weren't there?"

"Oh, yes," he yawned, "but there weren't even enough candidates to fill the few available positions allotted to grad students. It's hard to have much interest when there isn't even a modicum of a contest. Besides, graduate students ought to be asking what relevance the ASUN Senate has for their problems."[89]

"Perhaps they've already 'voted' on that issue," I observed. "Doesn't it say something about ASUN if grad students won't even run for the available positions?"

"That's an excellent point," said Leonik. "I think, at long last, you're beginning to get a genuine feel for grad student politics here at the University of Nebraska."

"But what politics can there be is students don't run for office?" I asked.

"Now you surprise me," he said bluntly. "Frankly, grad student politics involve issues that go far beyond the typical civics exercises of the ASUN Senate. When the time comes that grad students really close ranks on political issues, you can believe me it won't be to elect a senator to ASUN."

"You mean that grad students would only be satisfied with real political action?" I interrupted.

"You could put it that way," Leonik responded. "The fact is that legitimate politics are the only way to change the rhetoric of Nebraska's administrators into concrete accomplishments.

---

[86] *Daily Nebraskan*, 19 March 1976, p. 4.

[87] The Mill was then located at 427 South 13th Street.

[88] Scott's Pancake Shoppe, 401 South 13th Street, was a late-night, post-tavern favorite with geography graduate students. One geography grad student married a former Scott's waitress, and one geography professor conducted his evening seminars in a private dining room at Scott's.

[89] Pragmatically, the undergraduate majority in the ASUN Senate always outvoted the minority of graduate student senators five to one.

"For example," he continued, "when Executive Vice-President Steven Sample[90] took office in the systems administration, he said action should be taken to raise the average TA stipend to a minimum of $4,000.[91] That was two years ago. Where is the raise?

"A year ago, James Drew,[92] former Graduate College Dean, said he would like to see a tuition waiver for all Teaching Assistants. Where is the waiver?[93]

"And now it was reported in the *Lincoln Journal* that graduate TAs were commended in a recent Board of Regents meeting as being among the best teachers at Nebraska. Yet, do you think the Regents will reject the Legislature's 'gift' of $800,000 designated for the purpose of replacing TAs with full-time instructors?"[94]

"I begin to see your point," I commented.

"I hope so," he said. "And I hope that Nebraska's administrators see it too. If Nebraska wants to retain whatever status it has left as a university, then the administrators, the Regents and the Legislature must stop pretending that the only students at Nebraska who count are all undergraduates."

"Don't you think all this political talk is a little out of character with the traditional image of the typical graduate student?" I asked.

"Only because we haven't acted in the past," he replied quickly. "That doesn't mean we won't take concerted, meaningful action in the future. If real political action becomes the only way, many grad students will commit themselves to achieving substantive changes."

"And what about those who aren't prepared to make that commitment?" I asked.

"They may be the smarter ones, in the end," said Leonik dejectedly. "They'll just quietly finish out the semester, transfer to another university and never give Nebraska a second thought."

---

[90] Stephen B. Sample (1940–2016) was a personable and responsive fellow; he was later president of the University at Buffalo from 1982–1991 and then president of the University of Southern California from 1991–2010.

[91] In 1974, the average TA stipend was well below Sample's wondrously atmospheric proposal.

[92] Shortly thereafter — in 1976 — James Drew moved to Alaska to direct the Agriculture Experiment Station at the University of Alaska Fairbanks. Drew died in 2008 at age 77.

[93] Current practice at UNL now provides that tuition may be waived for Graduate teaching assistantships. The waiver currently has a value of approximately $7,000/year at resident tuition rates, or $17,000/year at non-resident rates.

[94] The so-called "Bereuter Amendment" imposed a cap on teaching by teaching assistants; see "Higher ed. Amendment approved," *Daily Nebraskan*, March 18, 1976, p. 2. It had little if any lasting impact.

■ 24 ■

Organization and Its Pitfalls (Formal organization idea rubs Leonik the wrong way)[95]

LEONIK greeted me with a relaxed smile and an unusual degree of composure. "Welcome back," he said. "Did you enjoy the spring break?"

"Yes," I replied. "You look like you had a pleasant time too."

"I went to Omaha with Yossarian. He's still looking for a job you know," reminded Leonik. "He took me to M's Pub[96] and introduced me to Irish coffee. It's the first time we've agreed on a drink that satisfies my preference for caffeine and Yossarian's predilection for alcohol. We also met a grad student from the University of Nebraska at Omaha, but that was a bit disconcerting," said Leonik.

"Why disconcerting?" I asked.

"Well, he had heard about the Vine Street Irregulars and wanted to know how to organize a chapter on the Omaha campus. Can you imagine!" exclaimed Leonik.

"Wouldn't that be a good thing?" I asked, surprised at Leonik's reaction.

"Oh, could be," he said. "It's the idea of *organizing* the Irregulars that upset me. The essence of the Vine Street Irregulars is that ware are *not* organized in any formal sense."

"But wouldn't you be more effective if you were formally organized and recognized by ASUN[97] as an official student organization?" I queried, hoping to baiti him into a political treatise.

"The Graduate Student Association is already officially organized and recognized," he thundered. "And you see how ineffective the GSA has become? Not that it's their fault. The problem is the amount of energy that GSA must spend just to keep itself organized.

"Every year, once GSA representatives are selected by each department, GSA officers are elected, committees are formed, reports are prepared, appeals are heard, funding applications are filed, and so on. After all that, GSA representatives have no energy left over to do the things that *really* need to be done. That's why the Vine Street Irregulars abhor formal organization. We don't even organize coffees, although I'm open to persuasion on that particular point."

---

[95] *Daily Nebraskan*, 2 April 1976, p. 4.

[96] M's Pub, 422 South 11th Street, in the Old Market, Omaha, Nebraska.

[97] ASUN, or Associated Students of the University of Nebraska, the "student government" apparatus at Nebraska, is dominated largely by undergraduate members of fraternities and sororities.

"But what holds you together?" I asked. "It obviously isn't formal organization that does it."

"Moral responsibility," he replied. "Let's take a hypothetical example. Suppose a few previously unacquainted graduate students meet at a party. Suppose further that they discover they share several serious problems related to graduate studies at Nebraska, even though they hail from different departments. And finally, suppose (a) they realize that an organized group effort could and correct their common problems, but (b) each grad has a different opinion as to what specific actions should be taken. Now, the question is: What should these grad students do?[98]

"What I suggest," Leonik continued, "is that these graduate students are morally required to form a *loosely organized* group that seeks answers to the question: What is the best way to approach our common problems as graduate students? Now, this is what the Vine Street Irregulars try to do. The Irregulars have not reached a consensus on what to do, but through discussion and research, we identify various possible avenues for concerted graduate student action. We leave it to the GSA to jump through the organizational hoops. In sum, we are neither *doctrinaire* nor organizationally moribund. Organization for the sake of organization is not our style.

"But don't people criticize you for being all talk and no action?" I asked.

"Yes, but it's misplaced criticism. Our purpose is not action *per se*, but open discussion, analysis, and research. What could be worse than taking action without thoughtfully discussing the question: What constitutes the best course of action?" asked Leonik, a relaxed smile returning to his face.

"Come on, Hilligoss," he said, "let's get a cup of coffee."

---

[98] What should these grad students do?; this is essentially the question posed by Virginia Held in "Can a Random Collection of Individuals Be Morally Responsible?" (*Journal of Philosophy* 67(14): 471-481) in a 1970 article I read at the time in preparing my subsequent 1977 paper on "Axiological Dialogue in Geography" (*Antipode: The Journal of Radical Geography* 9 (2): 93-96).

■ 25 ■

e pluribus interim (Interim student coalition — we could all go on safari)[99]

"HELLO, Hilligoss," said Leonik, a bit down in the mouth.

"What's wrong?" I asked.

"The department coffee pot is broken," he replied. "We have to drink *instant* in the interim. I know we have to put up with interim administrators at Nebraska but I always thought our coffee pot was a little more stable and reliable."

"But, Leonik," I quickly protested, "there is always flux in a university system: students coming, students going, professors retiring, and such."

"True," he admitted, "but it's a serious problem when the students are more stable than the faculty members and administrators. Just think about it," he continued. "We have an *interim* Chancellor, and *interim* Dean of Arts and Sciences, and an *interim* Dean of Graduate Studies, all at the same time. Since I began my graduate studies at Nebraska I've seen six different chairmen parade through my department alone!"[100]

"That does seem indicative of instability," I agreed.

"It goes deeper," said Leonik. "Take my doctoral supervisory committee, for example. My chairman is on safari in Shangri-La. One member is out on the lecture circuit this semester, and is hardly ever here. Another is looking for employment elsewhere and disappears mysteriously on job interviews. The fourth member will probably be here forever but he is only intermittently in touch with the real world. He at least deserves *de facto* interim status."

"People do move on," I said.

"It's not just the people, it's the system itself. When I got my B.A. degree in Omaha, it was still the Municipal University of Omaha, and Chancellor Hardin hadn't yet been rewarded with a Washington cabinet post for demonstrating that he could bully my Omaha alma mater into becoming part of "the Nebraska system."[101]

---

[99] *Daily Nebraskan*, 9 April 1976, p. 4.

[100] This exceptional volatility was, in fact, a day-to-day reality in one Nebraska department. Compare this situation to the former pattern in which department "Heads" served sometimes for decades, with the current model in which "Chairs" typically serve three-to-five-year terms.

[101] Clifford M. Hardin (1915–2010), Chancellor of the University of Nebraska from 1954 to 1969, served in President Nixon's cabinet as Secretary of the U.S. Department of Agriculture from 1969 to 1971. A key player in the creation of the Nebraska system was the

"You know, Hilligoss, I was adding up the number of years I've spent in what is now the University of Nebraska system. When I leave next year I'll have been in residence for a total of ten years. Why, a faculty member can't stay here that long unless he has tenure!"

"A personal education program that includes graduate school can take a long time to complete," I reminded him.

"True again," he said, "but it's supposed to be the students who leave, not the faculty members and administrators, one right after another. I've always thought you went to graduate school as a step upward to bigger and better things, but at Nebraska it's the faculty members and administrators who are stepping on us! They ought to rename this place STEPPING STONE UNIVERSITY in honor of all the administrators who have shamelessly used Nebraska as a means to their own professional advancement."

"Do you have a plan?" I asked.

"Oh, yes," exclaimed Leonik, tongue-in-cheek, "I propose a New Coalition of Interim Students! It will be our objective to be more interim than the faculty members and administrators. Unfortunately, the only truly effective way to fulfill this goal is to encourage students to *leave Nebraska before they get here*."

"Somehow I think that presents some tactical and practical difficulties," I mused, smiling at Leonik.

"Yes," he said, returning my grin, "but we can work them out as we pack our bags and our books. At least I've settled on a motto that's appropriate for this Bicentennial year:[102]

e pluribus interim!"

---

late Omaha attorney Robert M. Spire (1925–1994), a Republican insider who sat on the Board of Regents of the then Municipal University of Omaha. In the midst of that political skulduggery, I had the disquieting experience of sitting unseen in an adjacent restaurant booth one evening while Spire spelled out the deal to one of his co-conspirators at a nearby table: "Omaha joins the system, Hardin looks good and gets a cabinet post." Omaha's faculty members were, on average, more highly paid than the professors in Lincoln. The Omaha faculty tried, unsuccessfully, to block the "merger" of Omaha into what became a multi-campus system capped by an expensive, system-level administrative layer. To protect their salaries, Omaha became unionized whereas Lincoln did not, much to the disadvantage of the Lincoln campus.

[102] 1976 was the Bicentennial year of the United States.

■ 26 ■

Search Committees (The 'ship' is lost in the fog; where the heck's the CO?) [103]

"HELLO, Hilligoss," said Leonik despondently, plugging a dime into the Vendo-O-Matic machine in Oldfather Hall.

"Drinking coffee from a *vending machine*?" I asked incredulously.

"Everything seems to be falling apart," he replied. "The departmental coffee pot is still broken *and* we ran out of instant coffee today. I hope we can find ourselves a new chairperson soon. The position has been vacant since the first of January. Our department is like a ship lost at sea without a captain. There's no guidance, no sense of direction, we keep missing important deadlines. We can't even get the coffee pot fixed!"

"I assume there's a search committee to look for a new chairperson," I commented.

"Oh, yes," he responded, "I'm on it. The Dean thought it would be a good idea to have a graduate student involved in the selection process for our new chair."

"That's quite a responsibility," I said, patting Leonik on his revolutionary shoulder.

"It's also a lot of work," he continued. "The major problem is the faculty members that you have to work with. You see, engaging a new chair (or any new faculty member for that matter) always presents a department with two opportunities.

"First, there is a chance to give new direction to a department. Unfortunately, the departments which most desperately need such change stubbornly resist it. You see, real change threatens professors who were trained in now outmoded traditions—and who haven't kept up to date.

"Second, selection of a new chair or faculty member allows an opportunity to strengthen a department's program by adding someone whose academic interests overlap and supplement those of a current faculty member. If this is done carefully, a department can gain recognition as a center for the study of a particular topic. Unfortunately, many professors resent the addition of a faculty member with overlapping interests. Some feel that they are being 'challenged' or 'replaced' and won't be able to attract any more graduate students. And if you bring in someone *exceptionally* good, up-to-date, and innovative, the deadwood professors really feel threatened — with good reason!

---

[103] *Daily Nebraskan*, 16 April 1976, p. 4.

"So you see, Hilligoss, a lot works against you if you try to do a good job as a graduate student member of a search committee."

"It seems more involved than I first thought," I admitted. "Have you learned anything that would be helpful to graduate students who are selected for service on search committees?"

"I will make a few general points, " Leonik replied. "For example, remember you are a full voting member of the committee. You must shed the feeling that only the faculty members know best. Keep in mind that your job is to represent the interests of graduate students, not faculty members.

"You will have to work harder than many faculty members because you won't be familiar with many of the institutions from which the candidates send their applications.

"You must be on your toes to preserve the quality of the graduate program, and realize that the future reputation of the department may actually hang on your vote. That's a lot of pressure—and you have to be wary of professors who will try to sway your vote.

"When you actually meet the candidates, you may have to be the one who asks them potentially embarrassing questions."

"Tell me, are you enjoying your work on the search committee?" I asked.

"Oh, it's interesting, but I think someone like Yossarian would enjoy it more," said Leonik. "You see, each time a candidate is interviewed, the search committee gives a cocktail party so department members can meet with the candidate informally.[104]

"And frankly," Leonik opined, "I'm a little hung over. This is the sixth candidate we've interviewed this week!"[105]

---

[104] Not all departments are so open and, instead, try to insulate candidates from background information about the departments that inevitably surfaces during informal gatherings.

[105] This was no exaggeration. One large department was filling two positions simultaneously and appointed the same graduate student to both search committees. This was not only unfair to the student but also reduced wider student input into the selection process.

■ 27 ■

A Farewell Letter (A farewell to grad gurus sums up VSI philosophy) [106]

Dear Yossarian and Leonik,

    I'm sorry my farewell to the both of you must come in a letter. I had hoped that we could meet together at least one more time before I left the University of Nebraska, but it just hasn't worked out. It has been a good year and I have learned much about graduate student life from you. I'm sure that much of what you taught me will serve me well when I begin graduate studies of my own next fall.

    The philosophy and outlook of the Vine Street Irregulars have influenced my selection of a department for graduate work. I learned from you to look for a setting where graduate students can spend their time working to satisfy intellects rather than egos. You have taught me that a graduate program should be primarily an exercise in education, not in politics. But I have also learned that when a program goes sour, when it begins to value image instead of honesty, then vigorous political activism must be seriously considered.

    You have taught me to seek out professors whose reputations rest on quality teaching, rather than solely on long lists of publications. You have taught me that instructors must earn respect, not demand it because thy wear the title of "professor."

    I have learned from you that working with a professor should not require absolute submission or the forced acceptance of the professor's point of view. I will expect my professors to be open to innovation and honestly admit their limitations and shortcomings.

    Your have taught me to be wary of professors who will flatter and encourage me merely to bolster enrollments in their seminars. I have learned that caution is needed when entering a new department, that new graduate students are frequently "courted" by unscrupulous professors who want to increase their "following" in a department, and that new grad students are too often unwittingly enlisted as expendable pawns in departmental power plays.

    You have made me realize that not all my future classmates will be motivated by the desire to learn, that some will sell their souls, their integrity, and possibly their bodies, just to get an advanced degree. I know that there will be moments of bitterness when I see students who just "play the game" to get through a program or wrangle favorable job recommendations. Yet, I know that there will also be a few

---

[106] *Daily Nebraskan*, 30 April 1976, p. 4.

students, like you, with whom I can work and share the joy of new ideas, hard study, and honest criticism.

Thank you for this year of trust, comradeship, and sharing.

Best wishes,
Hilligoss

Appendix I

Selected Letters, Responses, and a Caricature

The Prophet [107]

Dear Editor,
    Reading Thursday's article [in *The Daily Nebraskan*] concerning the chancellor search committee, I realized my friend Yossarian is, among other things, a prophet. Last week Yossarian expounded on the nonexistent status of graduate students at UNL.
    Three students have been named to the search committee and not one of them is a graduate student. Everyone else was represented — undergrads, faculty, staff and alumni — everybody but graduate students.
    It seems very unfortunate that such a vital segment of the university community would be excluded from such an important task . . . . or was it planned that way?

                                  Give 'em Hell Yossarian!
                                  Francis "Hawkeye" Olivigni

No Exaggeration [108]

Dear Editor,
    In response to Michael Hilligoss's article on a graduate student's battle with university bureaucracy and red tape (*Daily Nebraskan*, Oct. 1), indeed it was no exaggeration. If anything, it is an understatement.
    The brevity of the article, with its focus on a single student's problem, tends to minimize the overwhelming sense of frustration felt by so many — graduate and undergraduate alike.
    But Hilligoss does touch on a very serious and menacing problem, and perhaps it is time to bring this problem to the full attention of responsible administrative and legislative officials.
    The bureaucracy, which has for years been a leading joke on campus, rapidly is ceasing to be amusing.
                                    Scott Greenwell

---

[107] *Daily Nebraskan*, 15 September 1975, p. 5.

[108] *Daily Nebraskan*, 6 October 1975, p. 4.

Guest Opinion: Inactive Officer Blasts Graduate Apathy [109]

Editor's[110] *Note: Richard L. Uznanski is a Ph.D. student and graduate assistant in the School of Life Sciences.*

I have been tempted to respond to the Vine Street Irregulars comments on graduate student life several times. I hesitated until I read the recent remarks concerning the Graduate Student Association (GSA). I am vice president of that organization.

I was elected at the April 22 GSA meeting. 30 graduate students, 1 per cent of the total, were present. After the sole presidential nominee, a political science student, won unanimously, he nominated another political science student for vice president.

I nominated myself. My platform was simply that I was not in political science. I won. Since that time I have not heard so much as a whisper from the president or any other officer.

Any executive committee action which might have occurred did so without the knowledge of the vice president. So much for the leadership.

The GSA is not a small club with a handful of members. Meetings are wide open. The only requirement is that one look old enough to be a graduate student. The few people who bothered to attend had full voting rights. (I have had nightmares about hordes of undergraduates showing up and taking over.)

The term "club" implies membership restrictions and duties. It does not apply to GSA. In theory, GSA has departmental representation. I do not know if this is stipulated in the constitution because no one ever thought to bring a copy to the meetings. It really does not matter, though, for the constitution was suspended more than a year ago.

The funding situation brought up by Hilligoss seems a minor problem at present. The $400 received from the Fees Allocation Board bought coffee and doughnus at one meeting and two issues of a newsletter, "The Grad Rag." (Compare with "The Yale Graduate Professional.") The total expenditure was something less than $150. Given that track record, requests for even $400 cannot be justified.

Major graduate student problems include restrictive library policies, student housing and personal finances. The GSA is supposed to be represented on the university-wide Executive Graduate Committee, the Lincoln Campus Graduate Committee and several other major committees.

Dean James Drew of the Graduate College seems willing to provide strong support to a viable student organization. The GSA has the potential to address graduate student problems from within the system. Realization of this potential rests

---

[109] *Daily Nebraskan*, 26 September 1975, p. 5.

[110] Rebecca Brite edited the *Daily Nebraskan*.

on the premise that graduate students are a broadly based, identifiable group of individuals actively interested in their collective welfare. This premise is unproven.

I suspect I will incur the wrath of graduate students for not doing my job as one of their leaders. They may have forgotten that I actually represent less than 1 per cent of their number. I need only apologize to the 1 per cent.

Perhaps my personal inaction has done some good. Last year graduate students received no coverage in the *Daily Nebraskan*. Now they do. Last year the executive committee pleaded for student support, input and involvement. They received little. Perhaps some of the apparent apathy is diminishing.

I had serious doubts as to the viability of the GSA when I was elected. Evidence to date has substantiated those doubts.

I commend the Vine Street Irregulars. They are raising and defining issues, something that could be done in no other way. As a side effect, they are relieving many of the frustrations I have felt with the GSA.

Richard L. Uznanski

Letter to the Author

To: Michael Hilligoss
c/o *The Daily Nebraskan*
City Campus
UN-L
68508

Dear Mike,

I really enjoy reading *The Vine Street Irregulars* column in the rag. I think it would be useful for future grad. students of "mine" (as the language goes). May I have xerox copies of each of your columns to reproduce for them. I advise about a dozen M.S. students and some of your work has been right on target.

Sincerely,

John DeFrain, Ph.D.
Assistant Professor
College of Home Economics
Department of Human Development and the Family

. . . and a Caricature:

Drawing of the author by a *Daily Nebraskan* staff artist
to accompany the weekly dispatches from
The Vine Street Irregulars.

Appendix II

DN Writer Is Now Sociology Prof — Rebellious 1970's Columnist Has Become Respected Scholar [111]

ELIZABETH POLLES
Daily Nebraskan

Michael Hill could be called a spokesman for the unrecognized and undervalued.

While working on his doctorate in geography at the University of Nebraska-Lincoln in the 1970s, he wrote a somewhat controversial column for the *Daily Nebraskan* in which he criticized many university policies and addressed the concerns of his fellow graduate students, who he felt were overlooked.

His column was a weekly report of the activities and objectives of an imaginary, underground graduate student organization called the Vine Street Irregulars.

He acted as an informant for one of the group's leaders, a character he created and named "Yossarian."

Hill said the complaints of the Vine Street Irregulars were actually composites of real experiences of people he had talked to.

Despite his dissatisfaction with some aspects of the university, Hill eventually became the only person to get two doctoral degrees from UNL.

Now he spends much of his time researching and editing books about sociology and teaching as an adjunct professor of sociology and geography at Iowa Western Community College in Council Bluffs, Iowa.

Hill's research gives forgotten but important sociologists of the past credit and a place in the field today.

Most recently, Hill co-edited a new book called "Harriet Martineau: Theoretical and Methodological Perspectives." The book is about Harriet Martineau, who is regarded by many as the first female sociologist.

The book has been nominated for the Scholarly Book Award, presented by the American Sociological Association's Section on the History of Sociology.[112]

---

[111] *Daily Nebraskan*, 7 December 2001, p. 8. This retrospective was part of a series "celebrating 100 years" of the *Daily Nebraskan*. The paper reproduced my inaugural VSI column along with this article by Elizabeth Polles and a then current portrait by *Daily Nebraskan* photographer David Clasen (on the back cover of this volume).

[112] As it happened, *Harriet Martineau: Theoretical and Methodological Perspectives*, edited by Michael R. Hill and Susan Hoecker-Drysdale (Routledge, 2001), received the ASA/HOS Distinguished Scholarly Book Award in 2002.

"(The nomination) means that your work is recognized by people who are really specialists in your field," Hill said. "It's very satisfying for someone who is a scholar."

Professor Miguel Carranza, graduate chairman of the department of sociology at UNL, directed Hill when he was working on his doctorate in sociology, which he received in 1989.

"I think (Hill) is very consistent and very meticulous in looking at those sociological pieces that have become, in some respect, invisible and forgotten," he said.

Hill currently is writing about several important and influential sociologists who worked at the UNL Department of Sociology about 100 years ago.

I'm trying to go back and tap into the ideas and values that these early sociologists were trying to work out," he said. "By and large, they were a very important group of people who deserve to be remembered and studied today."

Hill said that the discovery and exploration of ideas and the possibility of finding something new drives him in his work.

He also is motivated by sharing knowledge and making it useful to other people, he said.

A few years ago, he was given a grant from the American Sociological Association and the National Science Foundation to go the Library of Congress in Washington, D.C., where papers regarding the sociology organization were kept in boxes under restricted access.

He spent a year going through the boxes, deciding which papers to keep and organizing them so they would be available for research.

Hill said this project was one of his greatest accomplishments as far as being helpful to others, but his work was far from done. "A lot of stuff I'm doing is still in progress," he said.

About the Author

MICHAEL R. HILL, born in 1944, earned Ph.D. degrees in geography (1982) and sociology (1989) at the University of Nebraska-Lincoln. His former teaching posts include: Iowa State University, Albion College, University of Minnesota Duluth, University of Indiana South Bend, Iowa Western Community College, University of Nebraska at Omaha, University of Nebraska-Lincoln, and the University of Notre Dame. As the founder and editor of *Sociological Origins*, he is interested in the history and development of the social science disciplines and the fine arts. He is the author/editor/co-editor of several scholarly books and numerous articles. Hill is a recognized authority on the works of Harriet Martineau and Charlotte Perkins Gilman as well as the history of sociology at the University of Nebraska. Michael is now Associate Director of the Jane Addams Research Center in St. Joseph, Michigan. Recently, he was for five years a docent in the Krasl Art Center and is himself occasionally an active artist. Hill twice won the American Sociological Association (ASA), Section on the History of Sociology (HOS), Distinguished Scholarly Book Award (2002 and 2005). In 2003, Hill was honored with the ASA/HOS Distinguished Scholarly Career Award. He belongs both to the American Sociological Association and the American Association of Geographers, and is a full member of Sigma Xi, The Scientific Research Society.

The author in 2022.

Previous Zea Books

Michael R. Hill. (2016). *The Bureau of Sociological Research at the University of Nebraska–Lincoln: A Brief History, 1964–2014.* Zea Book No. 43.

Michael R. Hill & Mary Jo Deegan. (2016). *Dogs & Society: Anglo-American Sociological Perspectives (1865-1934).* Zea Book No. 46.

Michael R. Hill. (2016). *Space, Region & Society: Geographical Essays in Honor of Robert H. Stoddard.* Zea Book No. 48.

Michael R. Hill. (2016). *The Year-Long Adventures of the Blue Shoes and Their Friends: A Pedagogical Experiment in Visual Blogging and Tutoring University Athletes at the University of Nebraska-Lincoln.* With a foreword by Georgina Valverde. Zea Book No. 49.

THE END

www.ingramcontent.com/pod-product-compliance
Lightning Source LLC
Chambersburg PA
CBHW081328040426
42453CB00013B/2327